THE UNIVERSITY OF SAN FRANCISCO SCHOOL OF LAW

A HISTORY
1912 – 1987

By Eric Abrahamson

THE UNIVERSITY OF SAN FRANCISCO SCHOOL OF LAW

Published in the United States
by the University of San Francisco School of Law,
San Francisco, California.

ISBN - 09618081-0-1
Library of Congress Catalog Card Number : 87-50171
Manufactured in Singapore

TABLE OF CONTENTS

PREFACE

AS THE UNIVERSITY of San Francisco School of Law celebrates the completion of seventy-five years of service, it seems most appropriate to mark the occasion with the publication of a definitive history of the school, tracing it from its origins to the present day.

Each of us who has been associated with this unique institution, as teacher or student, knows only a small segment of its historical panorama. This history should enable each of us to place his or her own experience in a broader context, and to understand better the forces that have been responsible for both continuity and change in the institution.

The history of the USF School of Law is of course inextricably connected with the history of San Francisco, of Catholic higher education, and of legal education in the United States. To chronicle that history, we have been very fortunate to obtain the services of Eric Abrahamson, the editor of the California Historical Society's *Courier*. His skillful blending of events in the School of Law with events and developments in the surrounding communities produces a narrative that should enable all readers to see the school in a broader perspective and to appreciate its distinctive accomplishments over the years.

I hope that all who read this fine history will, as I do, find it a fascinating and instructive work.

—DAVID L. RATNER

ACKNOWLEDGEMENTS

THE HISTORY OF AN INSTITUTION like the University of San Francisco's School of Law emerges more out of the collective memory of its graduates, faculty, and staff than out of any single archive or library. I am most grateful to the many people who shared their time and memories, particularly Anne Quigley, Russell Berti, Francis Walsh, Delos Putz, Paul McKaskle, Vincent Hallinan, Vincent Cullinan, Albert Jonsen, Thomas Jordan, Stanley Walsh, Theodore Kolb, and Preston Devine.

University Archivist Michael Kotlanger, S.J., and law school librarians Virgina Kelsh and Marian Shostrom were extremely helpful. Gerald McKevitt, S.J., from the University of Santa Clara provided a copy of an invaluable essay from the Vatican Archives. Lindsay Kefauver provided photographic research.

Martha Brigham and her Law Alumni office provided much needed logistical support throughout the writing of this book. Christine Crawford, especially, was patient with constantly changing deadlines. Terry Ryan's proofreading was punctilious and sensitive. The fine work of John Williams, Barbara Ziller, and Timm Sinclair on the book's design is obvious. Dean David Ratner's support made this whole project possible, and he at all times encouraged me to tell this story honestly and candidly.

I am most grateful to Professor William Issel of San Francisco State University and Kevin Starr, who both read the manuscript. Martha Kendall Winnacker helped me to refine many of the ideas in this book. Most especially, I thank Father John McGloin, without whom so much of the history of the University of San Francisco would be lost. Father McGloin graciously shared his materials with me, read and commented on the manuscript, and saved me from numerous errors of fact and interpretation. Those mistakes that remain are, of course, all mine.

Most of all, I thank my wife, Lois Facer, for her patience and support during a remarkable year in our lives.

—ERIC ABRAHAMSON

FOREWORD

BY KEVIN STARR

A GOOD INSTITUTIONAL HISTORY must accomplish three tasks. First, such a history, most obviously and most importantly, must tell the story of the institution that is its subject. Second, an institutional history must relate the internal record to the broader considerations of the outside world, putting the institution into the context of its times. Third, and most subtly, a good institutional history should implode into its pages—by suggestion, indirection, and outright reference—a gloss, a metaphor, showing how the institution achieved value and identity.

Institutions such as the University of San Francisco School of Law are not just products of their era; they are circumscribed enactments as well, micro-dramas that show the part in the whole and the whole in the part. The true challenge facing institutional history is to treat the institution on its own terms, but to see in it and to evoke through narrative a story of more universal reference.

The following history of the USF School of Law, admirably researched and written by Eric John Abrahamson, masterfully tells the internal story of a school of law that since its establishment in 1912, has moved from crisis to crisis and from opportunity to opportunity. Abrahamson has organized his narrative around the polarity of theme and biography. The essential theme of his narrative is also a question: how did a school of law in a unique American city seek to fulfill its four-fold role of teaching, of legal citizenship, of institutional survival, and as witness to its Jesuit tradition?

First and foremost, the USF School of Law has been a teaching institution, keyed especially to the distinct needs of its upwardly mobile clientele. A goodly number of its most distinguished instructors have themselves been active, experienced practitioners, especially in the early years of struggle when full-time faculty posts were at a minimum. The USF School of Law functioned in those early years as a direct, no-nonsense way of introducing local men and women to the law—and the law to local men and women.

Second, as Abrahamson so deftly shows, this easy translation of teaching to practice and practice to teaching gave the school its first major institutional influence as its graduates began to dominate the bench and bar of the local legal community. Guided in its early years by Dean Matthew I. Sullivan—legal scholar, local political activist, chief justice of the Supreme Court of California—the USF School of Law was endowed from its earliest years with a philosophy and practice of committed legal citizenship.

Third, as Abrahamson also makes clear, the road was never easy. This history is in many respects a story of struggle for survival.

With candor and respect, Abrahamson has chronicled the frequent ordeals—financial, academic, administrative—that the School of Law and its protagonists seemed never able to escape. Despite the fact that it was officially commissioned, this history is not puffery or boosterism. This is an honest story about honest people, Jesuits and lay faculty alike, who often differed on the specifics of institutional direction. Abrahamson has made elegant use of letters, minutes, and memoranda in the USF archives to recover and re-present this exciting story of how differences were hammered out or, in certain cases, how differences resulted in repudiations and departures.

The very strength of the USF School of Law, its commitment to the legal training of the upwardly mobile, also resulted in one of its continuing difficulties—the failure to secure an adequate endowment. Not until the Kendrick bequest of the early 1960s was there a breakthrough in the matter of the physical and financial well-being of the institution. As this history amply demonstrates, survival was never easy. Today, by contrast, the School of Law sustains a sophisticated, successful development program, so that future deans and professors might never again be forced to endure the same financial difficulties experienced by the protagonists of this narrative.

The fourth and perhaps most interesting thread in Abrahamson's institutional narrative is the question of philosophy and values arising out of the school's Jesuit affiliation. More than any other school or college of the University of San Francisco, the School of Law has grown up under lay guidance and sponsorship. For years, a Jesuit regent presided over the School of Law as both the symbol and the substance of a continuing tradition. As a professional school, however, responsible for both its subject and the wider jurisdiction of the legal community, the School of Law of necessity bore witness to the values of its host institution, USF, within secular circumstances. Values could not be abstractly or diagramatically preached; they had to be discovered within the language and issues of legal teaching, scholarship, and practice. Sometimes, as Abrahamson suggests, this dialectic between theological and philosophical values and worldly professionalism was pushed to a point of strain. At other times, these polarized values galvanized each other; and the USF School of Law taught the law, not just as procedure and technique, but as a humanistic art and science dealing with the most awesome attribute of divinity, justice.

In the biographical dimension of his history, Abrahamson relates the history of the USF School of Law to its surrounding circumstances. The School of Law grew up at a time when state and national legal academic professionalism was on the rise. This professionalism was constantly reaching out to smaller schools—such as USF in its early era—and making demands. Year after year, the School of Law was forced to strain its resources to meet increasingly stringent standards of accreditation. It is one of the happy aspects of this narrative that these standards were, most often, not only met but surpassed.

An urban law school, the USF School of Law is unintelligible outside the context of San Francisco. San Francisco nurtured the law school in a special way, sending its most aspiring young men and women, many of them self-supporting, all of them willing to put in the extra effort to secure a legal education in less-than-privileged circumstances. In terms of public service, graduates of the USF School of Law returned to the city and added to the lustre of its bench and bar. Successive generations of San Francisco lawyers and judges were directed and empowered in their careers by their years at USF. When the city changed in the 1960s, the School of Law made adjustments as well; and a new generation, ethnically diverse, committed in a new way to the public interest, flocked to Kendrick Hall.

Implicit, finally, in this history is a subtle but consistent theme of the law, cities, and the young. Opening its doors to students on the fifth floor of the Grant Building at Seventh and Market, the USF School of Law was from its inception a vital part of the urban scene. For that first generation of students, San Francisco and the law constituted the twin goals of their impending careers. The city and the law served their desire for upward mobility, for a more complete use of their energies and talents. The most optimistic dimension of this history is the story of how—often after a hard day of work—young men and women (and some not so young) sat in lecture halls before committed teachers and first heard the language and intricacies of that mysterious, compelling calling, the law. One senses the presence of the young in and behind the institutional issues that dominate Abrahamson's narrative. One sees them in their stiff celluloid collars, freckle-faced and laughing, as they climbed the stairs of the Grant Building on that long-ago, long-lost Wednesday evening of September 18, 1912. One sees them traveling by streetcar out to the temporary campus in Hayes Valley in the 1920s. The echo of their voices still lingers in the fourth floor of Campion Hall and in the third floor of Gleeson Library. They came as returning veterans in 1946, wise beyond their years because of the war they had fought. They came in more privileged circumstances in the 1950s and early 1960s when an affluent generation first presented itself for a legal education. They came in the turbulent 1960s, their faces showing the full spectrum of the human condition; and they are there today in a vastly improved physical plant, learning the law from the most distinguished generation of academic professionals ever to teach at this institution.

No doubt the law will continue to intrigue the young as a primary and powerful mode of liberating talents and energies, of making one's life count—of doing the world's work. No doubt the USF School of Law will continue to serve this aspiration. A hopeful message emerges from the narrative that follows. Careers in the law are sought in each generation, and from each generation, lawyers emerge who commit themselves to lives of teaching and research. That interaction between the law professor and the law student, that sometimes tedious, sometimes galvanizing encounter, is at the core of any vital school of law. It is at the core of the USF School of Law, as this narrative suggests; and thus, whatever problems lie ahead, the heritage of this distinct legal academic institution, attached to a Jesuit university in a distinct American city, will ever remain relevant as a healing metaphor and a call to creative action.

CHAPTER I

FROM MANY BEGINNINGS

THE DAY WAS HOT—IN FACT, the hottest day all year, 94.5 in the shade. Through the open windows of the fifth floor of the Grant Building at Seventh and Market, the sun was setting beyond the city's western horizon. The sides of the brick buildings across the street, many of them less than six years old, turned copper colored in the fading light. The swirling white marquee lights on Graumann's Imperial Theatre came on. A newspaper boy below hawked the evening edition of the *Bulletin*. The day was Wednesday, September 18, 1912.

Dressed in vested flannel or homespun cotton suits, their hair parted on the side and slicked back, young men emerged from the elevator one by one. Their voices echoed along the hallway. Self-consciously they greeted each other. Most of them were old friends. Irish-Catholic, by and large, first- or second-generation Americans, with names like Fitzgerald, Fitzgibbon, Harrington, Kelly, Kennedy, O'Reilly, Mahoney, Mulcrevy, Murphy, Leahy, and Buckley, they came from the Mission or the Western Addition. Almost all of them had either attended or were attending St. Ignatius College, located since the Earthquake in what was affectionately called "the shirt factory" out on Hayes and Shrader streets.

For the boys of St. Ignatius, Golden Gate Park was a backyard playground. By the time they entered law school, many had formed deep and lasting friendships.
CALIFORNIA HISTORICAL SOCIETY.

Some, like Raymond Feely, William Queen, and James Harrington, were going into their junior years in the day school, completing their A.B. degrees, and starting the four-year program in law at the same time. Others, like Wensinger Mahoney and Francis P. Buckley, had already graduated and were starting back to school for their LL.B. degrees. Joseph Giannini ('11), star of the varsity baseball team, worked at the First National Bank while he went to school at night. Francis J. Mannix ('11) covered the Seals games as a sportswriter for the *Bulletin*. And somewhere among the crowd that packed the room was Chan C. Wing, who in 1918 would become the first Asian-American to be admitted to the bar in California.

Over the next few months and years, life settled into a kind of routine: reading the commentaries of Blackstone and Kent or *Robinson's Elements of American Jurisprudence*; studying for exams; waiting for the elevator at the break to go down to have a beer at Dierks & von Parten's bar, with one of the profs calling out, "Don't forget—one beer, boys, and come right back"; and when class was over, getting a pass into the 9:30 p.m. show at the Imperial Theatre to listen to the organ and watch the faces of Pauline Frederick, Bruce McRae, Ethel Barrymore, and Mary Pickford flicker on the silver screen.[1]

Located at the corner of Seventh and Market, the Grant Building survived the 1906 Earthquake and Fire and housed the offices of the Superior Courts until the completion of the new City Hall in 1915. At one time, both Hastings and St. Ignatius offered law classes inside the building's oblong rooms. CALIFORNIA STATE LIBRARY.

Despite the heat of that first day, it would prove to be an auspicious beginning. Of the thirty-nine students who registered to study law at St. Ignatius in 1912, twenty-four would graduate within four years, four more in five, with another three by the year 1918—almost 75 percent of the original list. Many would have long and successful careers in San Francisco; two, Harold Caulfield and Joseph Golden, would serve distinguished careers on the bench.

The story of the University of San Francisco's School of Law begins in a number of places. It begins with the Jesuits who founded St. Ignatius Academy in 1855. It starts with the Irish who came to San Francisco by the thousands, making up nearly one-third of the city's population by the late 1880s. And to a lesser degree, but in a quiet way, the law school emerges out of the history of the Progressive reform movement that shaped San Francisco and California in the early 1900s. As with most institutions, its heritage is its legacy.

When the law school began in 1912, St. Ignatius College had already celebrated its golden jubilee. Members of its alumni had risen to the highest ranks of city office: James Duval Phelan ('81) was elected mayor in 1897 and would be elected to the U.S. Senate in 1915. The school's graduates included some of the most prominent members of the San Francisco Bar—Jeremiah and Matthew Sullivan ('70 and '76), John S. Drum ('91), Thomas Hickey ('07), and Joseph S. Tobin ('87). If the list of prestigious alums was broadened to include those who had graduated from St. Ignatius High School and gone to college elsewhere, the impact of the Jesuits seemed even greater. In

Fifty feet from the Grant Building, Graumann's Imperial Theatre offered a welcome break from studies and work. CALIFORNIA HISTORICAL SOCIETY.

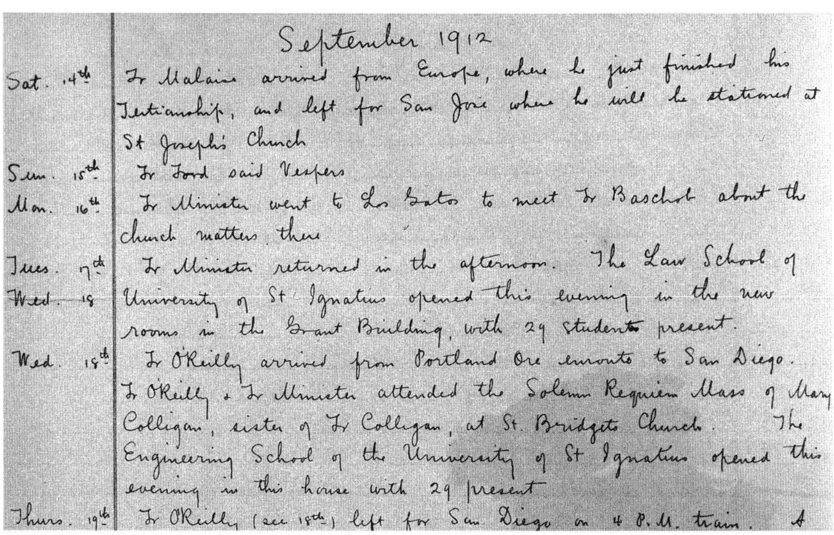

September 1912

Sat. 14th Fr Malaine arrived from Europe, where he just finished his Tertianship, and left for San Jose where he will be stationed at St Joseph's Church

Sun. 15th Fr Ford said Vespers

Mon. 16th Fr Minister went to Los Gatos to meet Fr Baschab about the church matters there

Tues. 17th Fr Minister returned in the afternoon. The Law School of

Wed. 18 University of St Ignatius opened this evening in the new rooms in the Grant Building, with 29 students present.

Wed. 18th Fr O'Reilly arrived from Portland Ore enroute to San Diego. Fr O'Reilly & Fr Minister attended the Solemn Requiem Mass of Mary Colligan, sister of Fr Colligan, at St. Bridget's Church. The Engineering School of the University of St Ignatius opened this evening in this house with 29 present

Thurs. 19th Fr O'Reilly (see 18th) left for San Diego on 4 P.M. train. A

In the house diary, the Jesuits recorded the law school's beginnings: "The Law School of the University of St. Ignatius opened this evening in the new rooms in the Grant Building, with 29 students present." USF ARCHIVES.

Father Anthony Maraschi, S.J., the founder of St. Ignatius College. USF ARCHIVES.

1912, the college could rightfully claim that "the sons of St. Ignatius [have] kept pace with the fortunes and vicissitudes of the city by the Golden Gate."[2]

Founded in October of 1855 under the direction of Anthony Maraschi, S.J., St. Ignatius Academy resulted from an agreement between the Jesuits and Dominican Archbishop Joseph Sadoc Alemany. For their part, the Jesuits had been in the business of education for 315 years, since their order was recognized by Pope Paul III in the sixteenth century. Jesuits had undertaken missions on every continent and started colleges throughout Europe; it was only natural that they should carry their vocation to the raw and rebellious city of San Francisco in the 1850s. Indeed, upon arriving in 1849, Michael Accolti, one of the first Jesuits to come to San Francisco, described the city as "a madhouse or Babylon . . . a soil not yet brought under the sway of human laws."[3]

ARCHBISHOP ALEMANY must have had similar feelings. Spanish-born and highly educated, Alemany worked throughout his career to rejuvenate and build the institutions of Catholicism in California. In 1854, in a letter to Archbishop Francis Kendrick in Baltimore, Alemany expressed his desire to see "a good college for the education of male youth"[4] established in San Francisco, and when Kendrick shared this information with Jesuit Anthony Maraschi, a philosophy instructor at Loyola College in Baltimore who had recently been assigned to California, the seeds of St. Ignatius College were planted.

San Francisco in the 1850s was a city ripe for missionaries and evangelists. Prostitution, thievery, and gambling were a matter of course. Fortunes were made and lost in a day by various kinds of speculators. The city itself nearly burned to the ground more than half a dozen times in the first ten years of the American era. Nevertheless, there were those who came for more than money, people who came to start new lives, even among the gamblers, miners, and fortune hunters.

Within almost every segment of the population, which by the end of the Civil War in 1865 numbered more than one hundred thousand, there was an almost feverish desire to build a great city by the Golden Gate. As individuals and as members of groups, no matter where they came from, San Franciscans tended to believe that here they could start over and succeed where they had failed or achieved less than perfection before. Each group—the Irish, the Italians, the Chinese, the merchants, the dockworkers, the Catholics, and the Protestants—struggled to define the city on its own terms.

On occasion these competing interests became openly contentious: the workingmen's campaigns against the Chinese and the capitalists, the teamsters' and streetcar workers' strikes, the verbal battles between Catholics and Protestants over the relative influence of each on the institutions of government and education.

This last conflict, in particular, played a considerable part in the establishment of the law school at St. Ignatius. For by the early 1900s, a number of Jesuits and other members of the Catholic community had become convinced that it was the policy of the state university, an institution which had its roots in the Protestant reform movement of the early 1850s, to effectively exclude the graduates of Catholic institutions from the

In 1880, the school moved into magnificent new quarters at Van Ness and Grove, across the street from City Hall. CALIFORNIA HISTORICAL SOCIETY.

university's professional schools, mainly by requiring a course in evolution as a standard of undergraduate education.

The view from the west over St. Ignatius College and City Hall before the 1906 Earthquake. CALIFORNIA STATE LIBRARY.

Within the community of Catholic higher education, this move solidified the growing consensus in favor of the expansion of Jesuit colleges into universities, collections of schools of specialized and professional learning. It lent strength to those who argued, like St. Ignatius Jesuit Henry Woods, that state schools were responsible for the growing number of Catholics turning away from the faith, that indeed the church had not foreseen "how serious would be the losses incurred by the Church through the attendance of her children at non-catholic professional schools, that have in the process of time become positively anti-christian."[5]

Consequently, as the latter part of the nineteenth century witnessed a general proliferation of schools of medicine, law, and engineering at major universities, partly in response to the increasing rationalism of the period, and partly as an outgrowth of internal organizing within the profession, Jesuit institutions began to follow suit. Indeed, when Father Albert Trivelli, S.J., announced the addition in 1912 of schools of law and engineering at St. Ignatius, proclaiming that "upon the formal introduction of these professional branches, the institution will assume the name UNIVERSITY, to which it will then be entitled," the change followed hard on the heels of a similar move at Santa Clara and was concurrent with the establishment of law schools at De Paul and Gonzaga.[6]

Within San Francisco, the establishment of a law school at St. Ignatius had particular significance. Like other Jesuit schools, St. Ignatius relied on support from the alumni and the Catholic community to make the new law and engineering programs a success. Understanding that status and prestige critically affected the new schools' abilities to attract students and get them work once they were graduated, Trivelli recruited two deans from the leading ranks of the professions: Matthew I. Sullivan for law and Michael M. O'Shaughnessy for engineering.

Matt Sullivan was a graduate of St. Ignatius. With his brother Jeremiah, he was one of the founders of the alumni association and one of the most active advocates of the college. It was said that he never attended social events other than University of San Francisco (USF) banquets.

Serious, highly moral, Sullivan had been involved in numerous Progressive reform efforts to clean up San Francisco city government. *The San Francisco Chronicle* credited him with breaking the political power of "Blind Chris" Buckley, San Francisco's powerful Democratic boss in the 1880s.[7] When

MATTHEW I. SULLIVAN

USF ARCHIVES

On Sundays, Matt Sullivan went to five o'clock mass and then walked from the Mission to his office in the Mills Building on Market Street. He worked until noon when his driver would pick him up to carry him home to 920 Guerrero Street where he lived with his brother John and his two sisters, Nora and Julia. From around the corner on Twenty-first Street, Sullivan's nephew-in-law, Eustace Cullinan, Sr., would come with his family to join the party. Sometimes from down the block, "Sunny Jim" Rolph would drop by, and they would all eat together.

It was Matt Sullivan, along with attorney Gavin McNab, who convinced Jim Rolph to run for mayor of San Francisco in 1911. Law partners with Theodore Roche and Governor Hiram Johnson, Sullivan was in many ways the workhorse behind a generation of Progressive leaders. He upset the political dynasty of blind boss Chris Buckley in the late 1880s, was appointed to the Board of Supervisors when members of Mayor Schmitz's administration were indicted, and, along with Hiram Johnson, succeeded Francis Heney as special prosecutor in the Abe Ruef trials after Heney was gunned down in court.

In 1912, after being elected governor, Hiram Johnson appointed Sullivan president of the Panama-Pacific International Exposition and then, in 1914, appointed him chief justice of the California Supreme Court. When his term expired, however, Sullivan refused to run for the office. According to some, it was against his principles to run for office. According to his grand-nephew Vincent Cullinan, "Uncle Matt knew he could make more money in private practice."

In 1912, when the law school at St. Ignatius was begun and Matt Sullivan appointed the first dean, there was hardly a more eminent lawyer in San Francisco, nor was there an attorney more committed to St. Ignatius. Graduated from the college when it was located on Market Street in 1876, Matt Sullivan, along with his older brother, Jeremiah (also a justice of the California Supreme Court), played a major role in the formation of the Saint Ignatius College Alumni Association in 1878. Jeremiah served as the first president.

Like Michael O'Shaughnessey, San Francisco's preeminent engineer who was appointed dean of the college of engineering in 1912, Sullivan lent his name and respectability to the new school at St. Ignatius but did not engage in the day-to-day administration. Nevertheless, he served as titular dean for twenty-two years until 1934. His contributions to the college as a whole were so significant—serving as president of the alumni association and engineering the purchase of the Masonic Cemetery land—it seems impossible that he did not play some role in directing the curriculum of the law school.

Married to his work and his causes, Matthew I. Sullivan died in 1937. *The San Francisco Chronicle* wrote that Sullivan "lavished his love on his city and his friends."

Above: A symbol of political corruption and graft, San Francisco's City Hall, which had taken more than twenty years to complete, crumbled during the 1906 Earthquake. THE TELEPHONE MUSEUM.

prosecutor Francis Heney was gunned down in court during the trial of political kingpin Abe Ruef, Matt Sullivan and Hiram Johnson voluntarily replaced the injured Heney and won Ruef's conviction. In 1907, when several members of the Board of Supervisors were forced to resign for accepting bribes, Matt Sullivan was appointed by Mayor Edward Robeson Taylor (then dean of Hastings Law School) to fill one of the vacated positions. Later, when Hiram Johnson was elected governor, he appointed Sullivan chief justice of the California State Supreme Court.

Besides his legal qualifications, Sullivan was a perfect figurehead for the new school because he commanded the respect of Irish Catholics throughout the city. He had grown up down the block from "Sunny Jim" Rolph. In the aftermath of the Earthquake, he and Rolph and Father Dennis O. Crowley founded the Mission Relief Association, which fed and sheltered thousands of homeless Mission residents. Sullivan is credited, along with Gavin McNab, with convincing Rolph to run for mayor in 1911, and throughout Rolph's career, "Uncle Matt" continued to be Rolph's closest personal adviser.[8]

It was part of Matt Sullivan's nature to work behind the scenes, taking little credit and little glory for the impressive projects he undertook for the betterment of San Francisco and St. Ignatius. According to legend, he refused to run for public

St. Ignatius Church and College fared little better. The building was not even paid for when disaster forced the Jesuits to rebuild again. CALIFORNIA HISTORICAL SOCIETY.

office "because it was against his principles." Indeed, he may be the unsung workhorse of the Progressive movement in San Francisco, which transformed city government from a patronage system into a modern, professional city management. Among other major pieces of institutional reform, Sullivan wrote the original City Planning Ordinance and Zoning Code. "Ever watchful of the interests of municipal ownership,"[9] as David Wooster Taylor describes him, Sullivan drew up the city's proposal to purchase the Spring Valley Water Company in 1914. In 1928, when the Jesuits wanted to purchase the Masonic Cemetery on Ignatian Heights in order to assure the future of the university, it was Matt Sullivan who led the negotiations and won city approval for the relocation of the cemetery.

In the bulletin for St. Ignatius University for the year 1912–1913, a number of men closely associated with Sullivan are listed as special lecturers on law. They include his brother Jeremiah, his partner Theodore Roche, Eustace Cullinan, Thomas W. Hickey, James V. Coffey, John M. Burnett, Frank J. Sullivan, James A. Bacigalupi, and Frank C. Cleary—Catholics all, and, with the exception of Bacigalupi, progeny of Irish parents. The core of this group was intimately connected with the Mission Promotion Association, with "Sunny Jim" Rolph's politics, and, more generally, with the interests of

Professor Benjamin L. McKinley and his Constitutional Law class in the Grant Building, ca. 1916. Despite his significant legal abilities, McKinley was less than intimidating in the classroom and was on numerous occasions the butt of student pranks. He is, nevertheless, remembered as a fine teacher. USF ARCHIVES.

municipal reform, the bar, and the Irish-Catholic community.

Judge Jeremiah F. Sullivan served six years as the president of the San Francisco Bar Association, longer than any president since 1880, and directed the transformation of that body from an elite club into an advocacy group, incorporating almost all of the city's attorneys and championing legal reform and professional improvement. In the twenties, following the legislative fight to create the State Bar, which was led by Eustace Cullinan, Jeremiah Sullivan was elected its first president.

Eustace Cullinan, Matt Sullivan's brother-in-law and neighbor in the Mission, was referred to as the "Colonel House" of Rolph's administration and was responsible for conducting many of Rolph's most sensitive negotiations. Theodore Roche, Matt and Jeremiah Sullivan's law partner, was appointed police commissioner by Mayor Rolph. James Bacigalupi became president of the Bank of Italy and was a leading advocate of regional government. Thomas W. Hickey, a St. Ignatius alum and Eustace Cullinan's partner, was chairman of the San Francisco Democratic Convention, which in 1905 attempted to oust Mayor Eugene Schmitz from office, and in 1928 seconded the nomination of Al Smith for president of the United States. Judge James V. Coffey and John O'Gara were both leading Democratic spokesmen.

It is hard to measure the impact of these men on the law school. Except for O'Gara, who actually taught regular classes, most were involved in their practices and their crusades, and their actual contact with the school was minimal. They were present at special events—banquets and graduation. From time to time, special lectures were organized that were attended by students, members of the profession, and faculty of the university; most of these men spoke at one time or another. The first lecture, entitled "The Roman Law," was given by Eustace Cullinan in February of 1913 and attracted a crowd that included Mayor Rolph, who afterwards praised the speaker and the faculty.

In many ways, these older alums, patrons, and sponsors of the fledgling school set the tone for the first generation of St. Ignatius lawyers. Their demonstrated commitment to the city and to the Irish-Catholic community fostered among the law students a fierce loyalty to St. Ignatius and San Francisco. They established a fraternity and a perspective that not only helped many a young lawyer find work, but powerfully influenced the shape of city government and municipal justice in San Francisco well into the 1960s.

Probably taken at the Ferry Building sometime in the early 1930s, this picture includes many of the men who oversaw the creation and direction of the law school in its first two decades. From left to right, standing: unknown, unknown, unknown, Eustace Cullinan, Sr., Father Edward J. Whelan, Mayor James Rolph, Jr., Matthew I. Sullivan, unknown, Thomas W. Hickey, Eustace Cullinan, Jr., unknown. Kneeling: James Smythe and Edward D. Keil. USF ARCHIVES/R. HAAS, JR.

PERNAU-WALSH
PRINTING CO.
PRINTERS &
PORTOLA THEATRE
30th ST.
STREET CLOSED

CHAPTER II

THE EARLY YEARS

FOR THREE YEARS, the law school held classes in the Grant Building on Market Street. The students watched the steel superstructure of the dome on City Hall take shape and then saw the building completed in December of 1915. In the spring of that year, ten students who had been accepted with advanced standing were graduated and admitted to practice by the appellate court on the motion of Judge Matthew Sullivan.

With the exception of the World War I years, enrollment in the law school steadily increased. Throughout the teens and twenties, the law school accounted for more than half of the total enrollment of the university. With few exceptions, the students continued to come from Irish-Catholic families—most of them the sons of first- or second-generation immigrants.

The success of the law school reflected the consolidation of Irish-Catholic economic and political power in San Francisco and exemplified the increasing sophistication of the leaders of the Irish-Catholic community. On the East Coast, an entrenched Protestant, native-born upper class had resented the

Market Street in 1918. In 1917, the law school moved from the Grant Building on Market to "the shirt factory" at Hayes and Shrader.
THE RECORDER.

Irish immigrants who came to the United States in the nineteenth century; the immigrants took the lowest and most menial jobs, they lived in shantytowns and tenements, and, worst of all, they practiced a "foreign" religion.

In California, the same prejudices were apparent—help-wanted signs were posted with No Irish Need Apply. But fundamentally, the community dynamics in San Francisco were different. As historian Robert Burchell has pointed out, "Because San Francisco had no past, because it looked only to the future, its development gave opportunity to native-born and immigrant alike."[1]

The St. Ignatius alumni who were involved in the creation of the law school were clearly conscious of their ethnic identity and extremely loyal to the institutions of their Irish-Catholic community. At the same time, however, they were often the most active and outspoken champions of the city as a whole and deeply committed to its general growth and development. Jeremiah F. Sullivan, speaking on St. Patrick's Day in 1886, captured the prevailing sentiment:

The offices of the American Irish Liberty League in the Mission District. Many of San Francisco's Irish-Americans were fiercely loyal to the Irish revolution. They attended rallies and gave money to the cause. CALIFORNIA HISTORICAL SOCIETY.

> It is not to be wondered at that the Irish people, proscribed mainly on account of their religion, should prize the mystic bond that holds them together in the embrace of an enduring nationality. To no one who has studied the history of Ireland can it seem strange that the Irishman's loyalty to his race and his faith should be blended in a manner so unique. It is not because the Irish Catholic does not understand and fully appreciate the relative allegiance that he owes to his government and his God. The Catholic citizens of the United States do not desire a union of church and State, a blending of functions essentially distinct. They do not wish nor would they consent to, the ascendancy of any church within the State. The Irishman would be the first, and rightly so, to resent the wrongs of a system under which he himself has suffered so long and so grievously.[2]

Lawyering was less a matter of precedents and theory and more a matter of advocacy and pleading. Even until the 1940s, many people would argue that the most essential component of a good lawyer was good breeding.

AS THE BASIS for Irish-Catholic political power began to move from the labor unions to the professional and business classes in the early twentieth century, it was only natural that the elite would seek to establish their own professional schools, in part to institutionalize their position. But in addition, as Robert Stevens explains in his book on legal education in America, "As the second generation of immigrants began to savor the benefits of rising living standards and free public education, the luxury of going on for higher education, once a preserve of the wealthier classes, became a feasible goal for some of the less well-to-do."[3]

Until the latter part of the nineteenth century, legal education in the United States constituted a period of apprenticeship and study under a successful member of the bar. Matt Sullivan, for example, had attended Hastings for less than a year and then was admitted to practice. Garret McEnerney, another prominent Irish-Catholic San Francisco attorney, studied law with the firm of Spencer and Henning in Napa before being admitted to practice in 1886. Lawyering was less a matter of precedents and theory and more a matter of advocacy and pleading. Even until the 1940s, many people would argue that the most essential component of a good lawyer was good breeding.

In the late nineteenth and early twentieth centuries, however, the concept of the law as a science whose principles are contained in precedent began to take hold in the legal community, especially among legal educators, and they began to promulgate the idea that a formal legal education should be a prerequisite to admission to the bar. In 1878, when the American Bar Association (ABA) was formed with the express purpose of raising the standards of the profession, one of its

Formed in 1878 as an outgrowth of the American Social Science Association, the ABA's principal purpose from the very beginning was to raise the standards for the profession and to promote the idea of the law as a science.

principal concerns was for establishing some criteria for legal education. As early as 1881, the association passed a resolution recommending three years of law school before admission to the bar.

But in these early years, the ABA had very little clout. In 1900, less than 2 percent of the nation's lawyers belonged; even as late as 1920, the percentage was still less than 10. In general, licensing came under the purview of the state and/or the courts, and many practicing attorneys, judges, and legislators resisted the elitism implicit in higher education, arguing that law school graduates usually had little or no sense of how to practice the law. It's worth noting as a sign of the times that at the turn of the century, there were still more lawyers in the country than college graduates.[4]

IN SAN FRANCISCO, the bar had been organized in April of 1872 to provide "more intimate and friendly association among the leading and respectable members of the Bar of San Francisco" and to prevent the legal charlatans of the era from "attaching their individuality to the general character of all..."[5] The organization functioned primarily as an elite social club, however, making little concerted effort to lobby for changes in either law, procedure, or legal education and having little impact on the public perception of lawyers.

In fact, the reputation of lawyers in general and San Francisco politicians in particular suffered considerably around the turn of the century when various cronies of "Blind Chris" Buckley and Mayor Eugene Schmitz were indicted in 1890 and 1907, respectively, for accepting bribes and selling municipal contracts. Around the courts and in the police stations, the situation was not much better. Among the more dubious characters practicing law, according to one St. Ignatius alum, was Jimmy Carroll, who "subsisted on half of the cash in the pockets of persons arrested for minor infractions of the law. The other half he offered to the arresting officer if he would change his story. When the police would not cooperate, Carroll would return his client's money and advise him to obtain other counsel."[6]

Thus it was not surprising that when the Bar Association of San Francisco was reorganized in 1901 under the leadership of Charles Slack and Warren Olney (both law professors at Hastings), the organization focused its efforts on improving the selection of judges and adopting a code of ethics. While there was much discussion about standards and concern for some way to keep out the "unqualified," this discussion focused primarily on character.

In general, the bar and the state made little organized effort to oversee the operations of law schools in the state. Consequently, the schools operated with pretty much a free hand in the early part of the twentieth century. A law school's policies were determined by the governing board of directors, the dean, or the net profit on the bottom line.

The city election of 1911. Backed by reform Democrats and Progressive Republicans alike, James Rolph, Jr., won the mayor's office by a two-to-one margin over Union Labor Party candidate P.H. McCarthy. St. Ignatius alumni who also swept into public office included Timothy I. Fitzpatrick and Thomas Lynch, both elected to police judgeships. CALIFORNIA HISTORICAL SOCIETY.

IN 1912, the prospective student of law in Northern California could choose from a range of schools with a range of standards. At the high end, the University of California's School of Jurisprudence (Boalt Hall), founded in 1903, and Stanford University School of Law, established in 1893, required junior standing in college and operated strictly day schools. At the low end, San Francisco Law School and Oakland College of Law, both proprietary schools, accepted anyone who showed up on the doorstep with the money to pay the fees. As late as 1933, a committee of the State Bar complained about the enrollment tactics of these schools "where commissions are paid to law students for each new victim they may bring to the school and where solicitors are not only regularly paid to hunt out and sign up prospects but are further compensated as long as their students stay in school."[7]

In this environment, the law school at St. Ignatius clearly found itself on a middle ground. Like many of the proprietary

On July 1, 1906, less than three months after the Earthquake, ground was broken at Hayes and Shrader for a temporary St. Ignatius Church and College. CALIFORNIA HISTORICAL SOCIETY.

schools, it sought to meet the needs of an urban, middle-class constituency aspiring to professional status. But unlike the proprietary schools and like those started by the YMCA in 1910 (now Golden Gate) and the Jesuits at Santa Clara in 1911, St. Ignatius did not seek to exploit those students but to serve them.

Admission to St. Ignatius was granted to anyone who had graduated from a college, university, normal school, or other institution with collegiate standing, or to anyone who had simply graduated from high school. Any student of the University of St. Ignatius who had successfully completed sophomore year could begin a law degree while finishing an A.B. degree. In addition, the university granted admission to special students who were interested in some specific branch of law as a complement to their commercial or political careers.

From the beginning, the school's orientation was practical, offering evening classes for men interested in entering the profession who could not afford to give up their jobs. The cur-

Eventually known as "the shirt factory" because of its resemblance to other hastily built structures south of Market Street, these temporary quarters housed the college and the law school for almost two decades. CALIFORNIA HISTORICAL SOCIETY.

riculum focused on the pragmatic aspects of lawyering, and the school engaged practicing attorneys as part-time teachers.

In the early years, the faculty of the law school was drawn primarily from the college's alumni, a practice that the ABA and the Association of American Law Schools (AALS) would frown upon in later years but which nevertheless served its students well. All taught on a part-time basis, again something not encouraged by the elite law schools, but characteristic of the vast majority. Among those who were there from the beginning and remained for a number of years were Benjamin McKinley, Joseph Farry, John O'Gara, Stanislaus Riley, and William Breen.

Among them, McKinley had graduated from St. Ignatius in 1893, earned an M.A. in 1908, and was appointed assistant U.S. attorney by his cousin, President William McKinley. He was active in the Catholic temperance movement and earned

By day, "the shirt factory" was filled with boys from grammar school, high school, and college. At night, the law students came to listen to lectures over the dull roar of the open gas burners that halfheartedly heated the rooms. USF ARCHIVES.

C. C. WING

MOULIN STUDIOS

When he graduated from St. Ignatius Law School in 1918 and then went on to pass the bar that same year, Chan Chung ("C.C.") Wing became the first Asian-American to be admitted to the practice of law in the state of California. Born in Napa in 1890, Wing was the son of a Chinese merchant from Sun Wu, a village near Canton. He attended grammar school in Napa and graduated from Lowell High School in San Francisco in 1912.

At the time of his graduation from law school, the Chinese Exclusion Law, first passed in 1882, was still in effect. Immigrants, particularly Chinese, entering the United States in San Francisco were detained at Angel Island for a period ranging from several weeks to two years. During the period of their confinement, they were interrogated by immigration officials, and their eligibility for entry was determined.

For fifteen years, between 1918 and 1933, C.C. Wing specialized in immigration law and facilitated the entry and reentry of hundreds of Chinese and Chinese-Americans. During this same period, the San Francisco police often accosted Chinese men, threatened and, not infrequently, beat them. Wing filed thirty different lawsuits against the San Francisco Police Department for harrassment. While none of these cases ever came to trial, Wing's actions did help change police treatment of the Chinese.

From 1919 to 1927, Wing practiced with two other St. Ignatius graduates: Thomas R. McGrath ('17) and Joseph F. O'Malley ('18). When O'Malley withdrew from the firm in 1927, Wing and McGrath continued together, their clientele growing continuously. In the thirties, Wing was appointed the first Chinese-American head counsel for the Chinese branch of the foreign exchange department of the Bank of Italy, a position that fueled his longtime interest in banking and finance.

At heart, however, Wing was a salesman. While still in school, he sold everything from books to greeting cards to photographs to mail-order men's suits. At seventeen, he began selling securities door-to-door, wearing a derby hat to make himself look older and therefore worthy of his client's trust. In 1937, Wing began phasing himself out of his legal practice. With partner Harry Wraith, he opened one of the first life insurance agencies in Chinatown under the auspices of Occidental Life Insurance. By 1944, the agency was among the top ten in the country for total volume and premiums, and Wing was well on his way to becoming a millionaire.

Throughout his sixty-five-year career, Wing was a member of the USF alumni association and maintained his friendships with several of his law school classmates. In the 1930s, he inaugurated a San Francisco tradition by sponsoring the C.C. Wing Classic Golf Tournament. One of his five children, Linda Chan, who has run C.C. Wing Insurance Agency since her father's death in 1983, graduated from USF School of Law in 1978, sixty years after her father.

Below: In the year 1915, San Francisco celebrated its phoenix-like rise from the ashes of the Earthquake and Fire. Created out of papier-maché, the Panama-Pacific International Exposition was a fairyland constructed to celebrate the triumphs of modern engineering and to announce San Francisco's arrival among the great modern cities of the world. PRESIDIO ARMY MUSEUM. *Right: A law school dinner held probably in that same year.* USF ARCHIVES.

the rank of colonel in the League of the Cross Cadets, a uniformed drill corps analogous to the Salvation Army. He taught two classes—equity and consitutional law. John O'Gara was an active reform Democrat who taught evidence. In 1920, when the grand jury was investigating allegations that certain police court judges were on the take, John O'Gara was one of four attorneys appointed by Bar Association President Jeremiah Sullivan to investigate the rumors and cooperate with the grand jury's efforts. Stanislaus Riley taught sales and served as assistant district attorney under Matthew Brady; he is perhaps best remembered, however, for launching a nationwide campaign that resulted in the widespread recognition of Good Friday as a holiday. Bill Breen taught probate and was later a probate judge and a partner in Matt Sullivan's law firm.

In the early years, the law school's autonomy was, to some extent, assured by its physical separation from the university. The faculty, for the most part, ran the school. Students took classes in the elements of law, real property, personal property, contracts, personal and domestic relations, torts, sales, agency, partnership, bailments and carriers, insurance, bills and notes, criminal law, corporations, probate, equity, constitutional law, international law, admiralty, water rights and mining, public service companies, evidence, and pleading and practice. In addition, Jesuit fathers offered instruction in oratory, logic, psychology, parliamentary law, and ethics.

IN 1917, the school abandoned its quarters in the Grant Building and moved out to "the shirt factory" at Hayes and Shrader streets. The shirt factory was a rambling, labyrinthine structure built to house the college temporarily in the aftermath of the 1906 Earthquake. According to Lloyd Burns, S.J., the shirt factory got its name because of its resemblance to a number of hastily constructed post-Earthquake buildings thrown up South of Market, some of which actually were shirt factories. By day, the halls were crowded with grammar school, high school, and college boys.

At night, for eleven years, classes of the law school met in the building's drafty confines. A number of men who attended classes later went on to achieve considerable recognition in the profession: Melvyn I. Cronin ('21), Raymond M. Greene ('26), George B. Harris ('26), Jordan L. Martinelli ('21), John J. McMahon ('25), Edward Molkenbuhr ('20), Edmund Scott ('23), William T. Sweigert ('23), William F. Traverso ('18), and Herman A. van der Zee ('22) all ascended to the bench.

Then in 1927, the law school moved again, this time to expanded quarters on the third floor of the newly constructed Campion Hall. For the university, this was the beginning of what would be a modern campus on Ignatian Heights. Negotiations for the Masonic Cemetery property, which would assure future expansion, were concluded in 1928 by Matthew Sullivan, representing the university, although a lawsuit initiated by several plot owners delayed the conclusion of the sale until 1930. In that year, symbolizing the expectations of the Jesuits, the students, and the alumni, the university adopted the name "The University of San Francisco."[8]

In 1930, the college celebrated its Diamond Jubilee. Father President Edward Whelan spoke to the assembled masses while Mayor "Sunny Jim" Rolph and Archbishop Edward J. Hanna looked on. On the occasion, the college adopted the name "The University of San Francisco." MONITOR FILES, ARCHIVES OF THE ARCHDIOCESE.

CHAPTER III

INCREASING STANDARDS

FOR A NUMBER OF YEARS, the California legislature extended to recognized law schools "the diploma privilege," whereby graduates of those institutions were admitted to the bar on motion. In 1915, the legislature granted this privilege to graduates of St. Ignatius College. But under increasing pressure from various bar associations who resented the privilege extended to the academics, were concerned about what they perceived as a decline in standards, and wanted to simply limit the number of lawyers in practice, the legislature in 1917 abolished diploma privilege to inaugurate a statewide bar examination.

In 1919, the California Supreme Court appointed the first Board of Bar Examiners. Sensitive to the controversy surrounding the institution of a statewide exam, however, the board was apparently reluctant to implement a difficult test. In the early twenties, St. Ignatius College graduates, like the vast majority of applicants, did well on the test. In 1922, for example, of twenty-four who took the exam, all but one passed.[1]

Fulton Street, 1926. Many of the graduates of the law school went to work in City Hall; in fact they dominated the city attorney's office for a number of years. SAN FRANCISCO PUBLIC LIBRARY.

Father Charles F. Carroll was appointed regent of the School of Law in 1925. As regent, Carroll substantially improved the school's facilities and library and hired the first full-time professional dean. USF ARCHIVES.

But in 1927, the passage of the integrated State Bar Act effectively transformed the State Bar Association into a quasi-governmental body with licensing authority. Those people within the bar who advocated a tougher exam and higher educational standards found it easier to argue their case among peers than among legislators. They could point to the 1921 American Bar Association recommendations, which called for a requirement of two years' prelegal college work and either a four-year part-time or a three-year full-time school program. In addition, reformers called for a "modern" bar exam, one that tested a broader range of knowledge. The Committee of Bar Examiners appointed to screen applicants to the bar implemented a much tougher exam in 1928. The pass rate dropped from 52 percent in 1929 to 42 percent and 43 percent in 1930 and 1931, respectively.[2]

Overall, increasing standards had a tremendous impact on the number of lawyers admitted to practice in California. Whereas between 1923 and 1926, admissions to the bar had averaged 796 a year, between 1930 and 1932 the number of attorneys admitted fell from 637 to 552. By 1939, the statewide pass rate on the bar had fallen to 35.4 percent, and only 254 were admitted to practice.

INCREASED STANDARDS for legal education in California paralleled changes in the bar examination and resulted directly from the increased authority of the ABA and the California State Bar Association. In 1923, when the ABA issued its first list of approved law schools, only Stanford, Berkeley, and Hastings in California qualified. Approval was based on four principal criteria: the requirement of two years of college study as a condition of admission, the requirement of at least three years of full-time or longer part-time study in law school, an "adequate library," and a "sufficient number" of full-time teachers to "insure actual personal acquaintance and influence with the whole student body."[3]

Until 1925, when Father Charles F. Carroll, S.J., was appointed regent of the law school at St. Ignatius, the day-to-day (or, more correctly, night-to-night) administration of the law school was taken care of by a succession of Jesuit directors beginning with John J. Ford, S.J. Carroll was a blonde, square-jawed, bulky man with a reputation for generosity and kindness. He was also deeply committed to raising the quality of education at St. Ignatius, where he had attended high school and college, and integrating the school into the mainstream of higher education.

When he became regent, Carroll inherited a school without any real permanent facilities and no full-time faculty. Almost immediately he began to modernize the school and, in so doing, to bring it up to the standards of both the ABA and the AALS. In six years, he solicited donations of over one thousand books for the law library. In 1927, Carroll oversaw the move to Campion Hall, and in 1931, he hired the first full-time faculty member—John D. O'Reilly, Jr. Under Carroll's administration, the first women law students were admitted and graduated—Bertha Ast receiving an LL.M. in 1930, and Helen I. Byrne and Anne W. Shumway receiving LL.B. degrees in 1931. Then in 1931, Carroll instituted a day law program at USF, which required a bachelor's degree as a condition of admission. Despite these changes, however, the increasing difficulty of the bar took its toll on USF graduates. In the early thirties, only 38 percent were passing the bar, considerably below Hastings' 70 percent, Berkeley's 79 percent, and Stanford's 84 percent.[4]

WITHIN THE COMMUNITY of legal educators, the pressure to raise standards was almost ubiquitous by the early thirties. But before the State Bar could adopt some rule for accreditation, some assessment of the current condition of legal education in the state had to be made. In 1932, the State Bar adopted a resolution directing the board of governors to conduct a thorough investigation of the status of legal education in the state and "of the entire problem of admission to the practice of law in California."[5] This resolution, in the aftermath of the passage of the State Bar Act, represented almost the first opportunity the champions of higher standards had for putting real teeth into their recommendations. Many could foresee the day when the State Bar would begin to accredit law schools and recognize graduates of only those schools as candidates for the bar examination.

To conduct the study, the bar empaneled a special survey committee and engaged two nationally prominent legal educators—Will Shafroth and H. Claude Horack. In the spring of 1933, Shafroth and Horack visited every one of California's law schools and reported on the individual school's strengths

Campion Hall as it looked in the late 1920s. USF ARCHIVES.

The graduating class of 1931.
PAUL VLAUTIN.

and weaknesses. Of USF, they wrote that the quality of education was rather backward, but was not bad and could easily be improved. They seemed pleased to see that the school's "ambition is definitely to put itself abreast of the best present-day developments in legal education."[6]

Specifically, Shafroth and Horack criticized the overuse of part-time, inbred faculty. "With one or two notable exceptions, they have carried along the methods of the school as it was in their own law school days, and have sought to apply the same means of presentation to the case system of study." Most especially, Shafroth and Horack thought the school needed a full-time dean "with modern law school training" who would be responsible for running the school. While they praised the uniform application of high standards for admission to the day school, they criticized the inconsistent application of standards to students in the evening division. Importantly, they politely rebuked the university administration for not investing more of the law school's revenues back into the school, money they claimed would have enabled the law school to hire teachers from "some of the better law schools in the country" who might establish a higher standard of teaching. Implicit in committee's report was the understanding that their recommendations should be the conditions by which the school would be accredited.[7]

It is probably a measure of Father Carroll's deep commitment to the law school that almost immediately after the survey committee's visit he began to search for a full-time dean. In the spring of 1934, he went east to Georgetown to talk to Lewis Cassidy, a relatively young but outstanding academic scholar. A graduate of Harvard Law School with a Ph.D. from Georgetown, Cassidy had taught at Creighton, Boston College, and Harvard, as well as Georgetown, and came highly recommended by the deans at Harvard, Georgetown, and Boston College. Apparently, the two men got along well. Carroll commented in a memorandum that Cassidy had "Catholic college training" and "close contact with ours for many years." He noted Cassidy's "exceptional ability to get along with others".[8]

When the job was offered to him, Cassidy asked for and received a four-year contract at the same salary he was receiving at Georgetown. If he had reservations about his autonomy as dean or about the difficulties implicit in taking over the administration of a school that had been operating for twenty-two years with very little change, guided by men who were for the most part old friends and colleagues, Cassidy must have been reassured by Carroll, whom he described as "a very sincere gentleman, gracious and understanding."[9]

The first women graduates to be awarded an LL.B.: Helen I. Byrne and Anne W. Shumway. USF ARCHIVES.

BUT AS FATE WOULD HAVE IT, on April 22nd, shortly after the deanship had been offered to Cassidy, Father Carroll died of a heart attack. To exacerbate the situation, Father President William I. Lonergan, who had authorized Cassidy's hiring, was removed from his office in July and replaced by Father Harold E. Ring, S.J. Thus, when Cassidy came to San Francisco in August, he found his position with the university administration already considerably compromised.

To make matters worse, Father Raymond T. Feely, S.J., had been appointed to fill the post of regent. Feely had spent almost his entire life at St. Ignatius, from grade school to high school through college and law school. He had been a member of the original law school class that had met in the Grant Building in 1912. He had been an officer in the alumni association, and Theodore Roche had offered him a position in the law firm of Sullivan, Sullivan and Roche. Instead, Feely had chosen to become a Jesuit and was ordained in 1930. At the time of his appointment as regent, he was a professor of political science and was already becoming a legendary figure at USF.

When he arrived in San Francisco late that summer, Cassidy was the stranger in town. In the eyes of some of the faculty, he had been imposed on the school by the State Bar Survey Committee with a mandate to make substantial changes: to raise the standards for admission, to strengthen grading policies, and to replace inbred part-time faculty with full-time teachers. Tacitly, Cassidy had the support of the university's administration, but practically, his position was insecure.

From the beginning, Cassidy felt uncomfortable with Feely looking over his shoulder. In the latter part of the first term, he complained to Father President Ring that Feely consciously undermined his authority and his relationships with the faculty. Feely responded to Ring by acknowledging that "most of the Faculty are either old schoolmates or old teachers of mine, and I presume that their chatting with me has given the impression referred to."[10]

Of greater importance, however, Cassidy and Feely went back and forth in memoranda to each other regarding the respective powers of the dean versus the powers of the regent, particularly with regard to the budget and the hiring and firing of teachers. Their standoff became particularly bitter in April 1935, when Cassidy did not renew the contract of Charles

RAYMOND T. FEELY

CAL PICTURES

For more than half a century, Raymond T. Feely was Mister USF. A member of the first class of students who attended the law school in 1912, Feely had virtually grown up among the Jesuits. He attended St. Ignatius grammar school in the early 1900s, graduated from the high school in 1910, the college in 1914, and the law school in 1916. While enrolled as a law student, he taught at "the shirt factory."

According to legend, shortly after Feely graduated with his LL.B., Theodore Roche approached him at the Olympic Club and invited him to join the firm of Sullivan, Sullivan and Roche. Politely, Feely turned Roche down. When Roche asked, "Got a better offer?" Feely replied, "Yes, a better one." Shortly thereafter, he entered the Society of Jesus. In June of 1930, he was ordained.

Feely was by nature a pugnacious and principled man. Between 1931 and 1933, he taught philosophy. In 1934, he became regent of the law school and also began teaching political science. He became a crusader against communism and fascism, writing speeches and pamphlets that warned Americans about German and Soviet aggression. In the mid-thirties he was outspokenly critical of Harry Bridges' leadership of the 1934 San Francisco General Strike. Then in 1939, he authored the University of San Francisco Credo, which affirmed the university's belief in God and its opposition to totalitarianism of any kind. Taking his zealotry one step further, in 1951 as academic vice-president, Feely instituted a required course entitled "The Dynamics and Tactics of World Communism."

Feely's influence on law school affairs from 1934 to 1956 was tremendous, and it was this influence that accounted for the departures of Deans Cassidy, Hogan, and Miller. On the other hand, his scheme for putting the university, including the law school, on nine-week sessions during World War II probably saved the school from closing its doors.

In 1956, Feely suffered a massive heart attack. Although he recovered, he was not again able to carry on the volume of work that he had maintained through the thirties, forties, and early fifties. His influence over the law school diminished. When he died in November of 1965, J. Edgar Hoover (joining others in the same sentiment) eulogized him by saying: "Father Feely was a noble servant of God and country and a stalwart defender of freedom. His dedicated life of service will continue to be an inspiration to his many friends and admirers."

Installed in St. Ignatius Church in 1939, the St. Ives Window was a gift of the St. Ives Law Club. Considered the patron saint of lawyers, St. Ives is depicted with scales and a sword at his feet, symbols of justice and truth. RICHARD CHATCUFF.

Knights, who was a graduate of St. Ignatius ('12) and had taught in the law school for fourteen years. Feely wrote a note to Cassidy criticizing him for his handling of the affair; Cassidy defended his actions and accused Feely once again of attempting to undermine his authority. He further reasserted his intention to build a law school "that will not cause me to have an inferiority complex when I sit down at the table to talk about Legal education with Dean McMurray [Boalt] and Dean Kirkwood [Stanford]."[11]

Despite the internal tensions, however, Cassidy's presence, the addition of three full-time faculty in the fall of 1934, and the university's promise to carry out the changes indicated by the 1933 State Bar Survey Committee, led the American Bar Association to offer provisional approval to USF's program in May of 1935. And in the fall of 1935, Cassidy hired three new full-time instructors (including Edward A. Hogan, who had recently completed his LL.M. degree at Harvard), bringing the total number of full-time teachers up to six.

Nevertheless, for Cassidy, the handwriting was already on the wall. He had made unpopular changes, and he was not regarded as a team player. Feely and Ring apparently made a decision to get rid of him as soon as the school received ABA approval. In a note to Father President Ring dated April 11, 1935, following a dispute over the selection of a speaker for the school's graduation, Feely wrote that "Cassidy still intends to usurp all the power we will let him assume. However, that's done too, so we can't do much till after the ABA meeting in May."[12]

Cassidy, indeed, seems to have sensed what was happening. He increasingly looked for support outside of the institution and its circle of friends and alumni. In November of 1935, when Dr. Brendan F. Brown wrote to ask what the law school was doing to give it a Catholic tone and to teach orthodox ethics, Cassidy replied with apparent impunity that those were "the least of my present worries." Cassidy went on to ask what responsibilities Catholic universities owed to their professional schools and sent copies of his questions to the deans at Harvard, Stanford, and Berkeley.[13]

Sometime around the turn of the year, Father Feely was replaced as regent. Cassidy claimed he was never even notified. In any case, he had already gotten himself into deep water. In December, he was informally censured by the conference of Jesuit law school regents who met in New Orleans. On January 28, 1936, Father President Ring demanded his resignation. Cassidy refused. Over the course of the next two weeks, Cas-

USF law school class in February 1934. SAN FRANCISCO PUBLIC LIBRARY.

sidy tried to save himself, soliciting and receiving resolutions of support from his classes and going over Ring's head to appeal to Father Provincial Francis J. Seeliger, S.J.

But on February 12, a special meeting of the board of trustees of the university was called. With the exception of two lay trustees—Matthew I. Sullivan and William H. McCarthy, who were both absent that day—the board was made up entirely of Jesuits. They considered and unanimously approved Father President Ring's proposal to cancel Cassidy's contract.

Thus the first professional deanship at USF ended unhappily for almost everyone concerned. Unfortunately, with Cassidy's exit, the conflicts over purposes and authority inherent in the relationship between the university and the law school remained and would continue. They were, indeed, fundamental and have become apparent in the relationship between most universities and their affiliated professional schools.

The law school, however, emerged from this era stronger than it had been in a number of years, and Cassidy deserved credit for many of the improvements. Reflecting the stricter application of admission standards, enrollments, particularly in the evening division, dropped 40 percent. Consequently, the pass rate on the bar began to climb: from 53 percent of the first-time takers on the September 1935 bar to 58 percent in the fall of 1936. Most importantly, in May of 1935 the school joined the ranks of a select number of schools in California when it was provisionally approved by the American Bar Association.

CHAPTER IV

THE WEIGHT OF HISTORY

IN 1903, WHEN HENRY WOODS wrote his memorandum to Rome, petitioning on behalf of the Jesuits for the authority to establish schools of law and medicine at St. Ignatius and Santa Clara, he asserted that "there can be no better means to preserve the faith of our professional men than to do the whole work of preparing them for their professions in an atmosphere of faith."[1] Woods argued that the public universities, especially Berkeley, were under the influence of the new university men (exemplified by University of California President Benjamin Ide Wheeler) who preached a "rationalistic and atheistic philosophy" and were "not merely indifferent, but also bitterly hostile to revealed religion."[2]

Woods decried the moral environment of the University of California where coeducation fostered immorality, fraternities parodied the serious rites of the church, and libraries were full of "dangerous" books. He argued that the fate of Catholicism and Catholic education in America hung in the balance over this question of professional schools. "Nowhere in the world do we find society more influenced by the doctor, the lawyer, the professor, than here in America," he wrote.

Under construction in the middle 1930s, the Golden Gate Bridge towers stood isolated and unconnected in 1936. Completed a year later, the bridge became the most recognizable symbol of San Francisco. CALIFORNIA HISTORICAL SOCIETY.

"Therefore to influence American society, sorely in need of wholesome, christian influences, we must oppose to doctrinaires a body of professional men and professors imbued with right principles."[3]

Nine years later, when schools were established at Santa Clara and St. Ignatius, "the atmosphere of faith" would underlie the Jesuit approach to legal education. The Jesuits promised to "give the youth committed to their charge the higher mental culture" and to "spare no effort to form them also to habits of virtue."[4] No course in religion, philosophy, or ethics was listed in the law school curriculum, but Father Denis J. Mahony, S.J., was listed under the faculty as "Special Lecturer on Philosophy in the College of Law." And older alumni, veterans of "the shirt factory" era, remember a Thursday night course in ethics and philosophy, taught by Fathers Foote, Cunningham, and—the great orator himself—Cavanaugh, which was required for all students who were not enrolled in the day program of the college. As Woods had pointed out, it was the environment of the school that was supposed to inculcate and support a moral, civically minded, Catholic perspective.

Known as "the great orator," Father Dennis Cavanaugh packed the pews of St. Ignatius when he was scheduled to give a sermon. Occasionally, Cavanaugh taught ethics in the law school and throughout his life was concerned with principles of justice. MONITOR FILES, ARCHIVES OF THE ARCHDIOCESE/WIDE WORLD PHOTOS.

WOODS HAD WARNED that without professional schools, Catholic universities would have to surrender their curriculum to the state university men, and become subject to a state-run accreditation process, to enable students of Catholic schools to gain admittance to public professional schools. If that happened, "Every enemy of Catholic education would welcome it," he wrote, "and most of all the University authorities themselves, as a complete surrender of Catholic education into their hands."[5]

Woods' words were prophetic. Accreditation did come, but the establishment of Catholic professional schools did not protect the autonomy of Catholic higher education from the forces of rationalism and professionalism. It was, after all, difficult for Jesuit fathers to administer a law school unless they had training in the profession. And throughout the twenties, thirties, and forties, the organized bar gained more and more authority. The State Bar Survey Committee's recommendation, for example, that USF hire a full-time dean of the law school carried tremendous weight, especially because it was implicitly tied to any eventual approval by the ABA or eventual accreditation by the State Bar. Practically, the increasing influence of the bar on the operation of the law school began to compromise the administrative authority of the Jesuits.

The summer after Cassidy was dismissed, he wrote a long memorandum to the ABA and the State Bar, complaining about the treatment he had received at USF and criticizing especially the regent/dean administrative structure of the law school. Cassidy characterized the position of the regent as "peculiar," and, indeed, it was a particularly Catholic administrative structure, present in most of the Jesuit law schools.[6]

The regent's job was to monitor the operation of the school, making sure that its policies were consonant with the general philosophies and procedures of the university and the Jesuit order. He was to be the Jesuit liaison between the dean and the president, responsible for the amount of the budget, but not for its expenditure. From the Jesuit perspective, the creation of the regent/dean structure reflected a legitimate compromise of authority.

Benjamin Ide Wheeler became president of the University of California in 1899. He was the first of what Thomas Barnes has called "the imperial presidents" of the university. Among other things, Wheeler championed evolution and the rational social sciences and thereby earned the enmity of some members of the Jesuit community. BANCROFT LIBRARY.

In fact, the position of the regent was problematic. In 1954, in a speech before the Association of Jesuit Law Schools, John G. Hervey, a prominent legal educator, pointedly asked, "Do not the church Fathers trust the lay administrators? Why should you entrust things monetary to the Regent rather than to the Dean? Will not the one with the stronger personality dominate the faculty and dictate school policies?"[7]

A graduate of the law school class of 1927, Preston Devine went on to teach at USF for a number of years before being appointed to the bench in 1946 by Governor Earl Warren. Sitting on either side are Garret McEnerney, II and Howard Finn. USF ARCHIVES.

BETWEEN CASSIDY AND FEELY, Feely's was the stronger personality, and he did dominate. To be fair, however, he was perhaps as uncomfortable with this balance of power as Cassidy. He had no model. Matt Sullivan was not an administrative dean, and Father Carroll's administrative authority was undisputed, except by the university president. When tensions between Cassidy and Feely became particularly acute, Feely asked Father President Ring how these problems were addressed at Georgetown or any of the other Catholic schools that utilized the regent system. If he got an answer, it was apparently not a solution. He appears to have struggled to find a balance between his sense of duty, his respect for Cassidy's position, and his allegiance to his old friends, schoolmates, and faculty peers.

In the end, it was perhaps this conflicting sense of loyalty that brought Cassidy and Feely into deepest conflict. While Cassidy may have been overambitious and lacked the confidence to handle his difficult position at USF, he was perhaps most guilty in the institutional context of having first loyalties that extended beyond USF and San Francisco. He naturally allied himself with Harvard and with the elite academic legal educators who had trained him. His ambitions were for himself and for the law school. As Father Feely concluded in a note written to him in April of 1935, "You are sincerely trying to build up the School of Law. I evaluate the Law School as a part of USF. Some day I trust we can see eye to eye."[8]

In some ways, Feely and Cassidy were not far apart. Both Jesuit and lay faculty and staff of the law school and the university worked hard throughout the thirties to win the approval of the ABA (1935), the AALS (1937), and the State Bar (1937). In doing so, they conformed the school more and more to the standards of the profession of legal educators.

For the Jesuits, the creation of "an atmosphere of faith" in the law school became something of a rear-guard action.

The approach to the law as an objective science became more pervasive, became in fact an implicit value by which one's professionalism was measured, and—as Woods had predicted—tended to undermine all other faiths.

In the aftermath of the eighteen-month Cassidy affair, the university authorities tried to come to terms with the law school's relationship to the university and to Jesuit education in general. After John O'Reilly was appointed interim dean in February, Father President Ring wrote him a memorandum intended "to define and clarify the relation between the School of Law and the other departments of the University." Ring made it clear that the law school was "an integral, but autonomous school of the University, under the direction of the Dean in all internal affairs," but went on to state that the school and the dean were "under the obligation of co-operating, in matters involving the interest of the University. . . "[9]

. . . the* Bulletin of the School of Law *for 1936–37 stated that the school existed "to train students in the principles of the Common Law," and, in addition, "to break away from an insularity which in America has resulted in lawyers having little legal philosophy not predicated upon the Common Law". . .

TO CLARIFY THE PURPOSES of the law school within the context of a Jesuit university, the *Bulletin of the School of Law* for 1936–1937 stated that the school existed "to train students in the principles of the Common Law," and, in addition, "to break away from an insularity which in America has resulted in lawyers having little legal philosophy not predicated upon the Common Law"—in other words, to teach values, as well as the law. "A lawyer with an analytical mind," the *Bulletin* continued, "and a knowledge of legal precedents will not be a complete lawyer if in his practice he does not realize his debt to society and his profession, and manifest in his practice the highest ethical standards."[10] The statement was unusual not so much for what it said but for the fact that it had to be said at all.

The changes initiated by Father Carroll had been furthered by Feely and Cassidy and finally came to fruition under the deanship of Charles H. Kinnane. Hired in 1936, Kinnane came from the law school of the University of Wyoming, where he had been dean. He was a graduate of Yale and, among other accomplishments, was the author of a general text on Anglo-American Law, a book that had evolved out of an Introduction to Law course he had taught at Wyoming.

Kinnane's perspective was well-suited to a Jesuit environment. As an academic, he favored a broad approach and was deeply concerned about social justice. In the second edition to his book, published in 1952, twenty years after it had first appeared, Kinnane added a preface that emphasized his belief that "an American lawyer should be able to see his legal system as a whole, and in relation to other legal systems, for in no other way is he likely to become able to see the law for what it is, namely an instrument for the practical solution, whether well or badly, of the universal and timeless problems of human social living."[11]

The logo of the St. Ives Law Club. Founded in October of 1934 by Professor A. Russell Berti, the St. Ives Law Club was for USF undergraduates interested in going into law. Among other activities, the club sponsored lectures and field trips to various legal and governmental institutions.
USF ARCHIVES.

KINNANE STATED THAT the law and the practice of the law were reflections of values, and if anything, he appears to have become increasingly suspicious of the concept of law as a science. "Man is forever faced," he wrote, "... with that matter of competing solutions and of choice between them. This should be thoroughly understood, but not merely with the surface of the mind. Such understanding should be completely pervasive; it should penetrate to every aspect of thinking about legal matters."[12]

When he took over the deanship at USF, Kinnane set out to solidify the improvements his predecessors had undertaken and specifically set his sights on winning membership in the AALS. In 1937, the law school became one of five schools in the state to be admitted to the association and was the only law school in San Francisco approved by either the AALS or the ABA. (Hastings had been dropped from the AALS in 1927 and did not regain admission until 1947.) That same year, when the California Committee of Bar Examiners began accrediting law schools, USF gained accreditation easily.

Kinnane apparently enjoyed the full support of the university administration, and his relationships with the regent, Father Cornelius Buckley, Father President Harold Ring, and Father William J. Dunne (Ring's successor) were apparently quite amicable. His awareness of, and concern for, the alumni were apparent in the fact that he began publishing an annual newsletter and report addressed to the alumni of the law school.

Kinnane aspired to establish USF in the first rank of schools. Publicly, he proudly reported to the alumni and the president of the university in the spring of 1938 that the number of volumes in the law library exceeded ABA requirements by 80 percent and that the number of full-time teachers was twice what the ABA required. On the bar exam, the school had risen from twelfth place in 1934 to sixth place in 1937 with an overall pass rate of more than 60 percent, and students whose grade points were C+ or higher had a pass rate of more than 82 percent. "Since the adoption five years ago of the new policies in regard to the school," wrote Kinnane in his conclusion, "there has been no disposition to be content with merely grudging, or formal compliance with minimum requirements." According to Kinnane, every provision had been made to assure the school's future as a school of "the highest character."[13]

Economically, however, the 1930s were as difficult for USF as they were for the nation. The university had celebrated its diamond jubilee in 1930, and in 1934 finally concluded the acquisition of the Masonic Cemetery property, but not without increasing the university's debt considerably. At the diamond jubilee, Matthew I. Sullivan had outlined grand plans for the university's expansion on Ignatian Heights, but by the middle 1930s it became obvious that it would be a long time before the university would have the capital to begin construction.

The General Strike of 1934, an outgrowth of the International Longshoremen's Association strike, effectively shut down San Francisco for four days. Several of the faculty members at USF actively opposed the "radicalism" of San Francisco's labor movement in the 1930s. ILWU, THE DISPATCHER.

VINCENT HALLINAN

THE RECORDER

When he passed the bar in 1920 after completing fewer than half of his law courses at St. Ignatius, Vincent Hallinan became the youngest attorney in San Francisco. Sixty-seven years later, at the age of ninety, Hallinan is still practicing true to form in San Francisco—judge-baiting and crusading on behalf of his clients and his ideals.

Above all, Vincent Hallinan is a fighter. His image of himself, even at ninety, seems to be embodied in the "Ripley's Believe It or Not" picture that hangs in his office: Hallinan as a young man in a tiger's stance, fingers spread wide, ready for all adversaries—"the Iron Man of Football." "I was a roughneck," he says simply.

He began as the "boy orator" of the Irish rebels of San Francisco, speaking out in San Francisco Civic Auditorium in support of the rebellion in Ireland. A St. Ignatius product nearly all the way, Hallinan graduated from the high school, the college, and the law school and wrote prolifically for the *Ignatian*, frequently filling blank pages with poems composed on his streetcar rides to the printer.

Hallinan made his name in San Francisco's legal community as a rebel and a risk taker. In 1932, he defended accused murderer Frank Egan against remarkable odds and managed to win for Egan a life sentence instead of execution. In 1945, he took the celebrated case of Irene Mansfeldt, who was accused of murdering a nurse Mansfeldt believed was having an affair with her husband. Despite Mansfeldt's detailed confession given to the press moments after the shooting, Hallinan won for his client a manslaughter verdict.

In the 1950s, Hallinan turned his full attention to leftist politics, defending labor organizer Harry Bridges against U.S. Immigration efforts to have Bridges expelled from the country for being a communist. When Henry Wallace abandoned the Progressive Party he and others had created to challenge Truman and Dewey in the 1948 presidential campaign, Hallinan was nominated by the Progressives to run for president of the United States in 1952. Hallinan, however, spent the bulk of the campaign in jail, cited for contempt of court in the Harry Bridges case. Nevertheless, in November, he and running mate Charlotta Bass garnered 140,000 votes in the twenty-four states where they were on the ballot.

Despite his electoral defeat, Hallinan continued to defend the interests of minorities and protestors in the late fifties, sixties, and seventies, sharing his crusade with his wife Vivian and their six sons. When his son Terrence was refused admission to the bar despite having passed the exam, Hallinan sued and won. In the process, however, he was once more cited for contempt. In response, at the age of seventy-six, Hallinan campaigned against that particular judge for his Superior Court seat.

Hallinan continues to be a fighter. Nevertheless, as anyone who knows him will testify, he combines remarkable pragmatism and resourcefulness with a continuing idealism. He has defined a courtroom style that is practically a San Francisco tradition.

Throughout the decade, the law school remained quartered on the third floor of Campion Hall; students were able to look out through the windows to the west, over the top of the Jesuit's residence (razed in 1966), to the twin towers of St. Ignatius Church. Rising standards in the law school meant more selective admissions, and registrations in both the day and evening divisions, which had numbered 197 in 1935, dropped to 114 in 1939. The number of degrees awarded in law declined from an average of over 50 a year at the end of the twenties to only 17 at the end of the decade.

"Strike Called Off." After paralyzing the city for four days, the General Strike ended on July 27, 1934, when both sides agreed to arbitration. CALIFORNIA HISTORICAL SOCIETY.

In the fall of 1938, Kinnane addressed a memorandum to Fathers Dunne and Buckley, expressing his desire to begin renegotiating his contract, which would expire in the summer of 1939. Before doing so, he said, he wanted to get some sense of the university's plans for the school's future. He mentioned rumors that the school was going to be abolished and flatly stated that he had no interest in acting "as undertaker for a soon-to-be-defunct enterprise."[14]

Kinnane asserted that the main job he had been hired for—bringing the school up to the minimum standards of the profession—had been accomplished. He asked whether the university was willing to make the kind of commitment that would enable the school to go to the next level. "We now have

Margaret Proctor came to St. Ignatius in 1928. She served as registrar, secretary, and, in many ways, the eminence grise *to various deans of the law school for twenty-eight years.* USF ARCHIVES.

constructed a foundation...," he added. "I do not think however, that we have done anything about the superstructure as yet... We are, so to speak, 'holding church in the basement'"[15] Bravely, Kinnane stated that if construction of the superstructure was about to begin, he would like to be invited to stay on. If, however, the school was to endure "a long continued process of suspended animation," then he would prefer to go elsewhere.

THROUGHOUT THE FALL and winter of 1938–1939, Kinnane wrote long memoranda to Father President Dunne, highlighting opportunities he saw for improving the school. One of these was the suggestion that USF purchase the hard-pressed San Francisco Law School and take over its facilities. Kinnane's letters were answered for the most part with silence. Dunne's health was not good, and the university's economic status was uncertain.

Finally, on February 15, 1939, Father President Dunne wrote a brief note to Kinnane informing the dean that the university would not purchase the San Francisco Law School, that another full-time professor could not be engaged, that there was no money available for an additional twenty-three scholarships, and that "in view of the financial condition of the Law School at present and the indications for the future," Kinnane's request for a raise would not be granted. The next day Kinnane regretfully tendered his resignation.[16]

Despite his early resolve, however, Kinnane equivocated, and at one point, in a moment of sentiment, he asked to stay on, even offering part of his own salary to enable the university to give raises to other members of the law school faculty. He had clearly grown attached to the school and the city and was enamored of the Jesuits and their philosophy. Appreciating Kinnane's gesture, Father President Dunne, nevertheless, did not accept Kinnane's offer.

Before leaving USF, Kinnane wrote to both the ABA and the AALS, reporting on the progress of the school during the tenure of his deanship, and stating categorically that he was choosing to move on for personal reasons and not for lack of support from the university. When he left USF after graduation in June of 1939, he went on to a job at De Paul University, and in 1941, he narrowly missed being appointed to the deanship of Hastings, losing out to the legendary David E. Snodgrass.

Opening day on the Golden Gate Bridge—May 27, 1937. CALIFORNIA HISTORICAL SOCIETY.

Underwood

CHAPTER V

POLITICS, IDEALS, AND THE NATION AT WAR

CHARLES KINNANE HAD FEARED that the law school was about to enter a long period of suspended animation. In fact, in 1939 the whole country seemed to be in suspended animation. The rise of fascism in Europe, the accumulated effects of the Great Depression and the New Deal in the United States, combined with the increasing success and consolidation of the labor movement around the country and in San Francisco, gave rise to a feeling that a new world order was in the making.

At USF, the political mood tended to be conservative, suspicious of the New Deal and of organized labor, strongly in favor of individual liberties, and outspokenly demanding regarding the civic responsibilities of both labor and capital. In 1939, Father Raymond Feely, an outspoken critic of communism, drafted the USF Credo, which was published on February 23, 1940. Among other things, the credo asserted, "We believe that man has natural rights which come from God and not from the state. We are therefore opposed to all forms of dictatorship which are based on the philosophy that the 'total man' (totalitarianism) belongs to the state."[1] The publication of the credo attracted national attention and earned the

Within weeks of the attack on Pearl Harbor, a recruiting office was opened at the Palace Hotel, and young men, some of them USF students, stood in line to enlist. SAN FRANCISCO PUBLIC LIBRARY.

university a reputation as a strongly anti-communist institution—a reputation that would be furthered substantially in the 1950s when, at Feely's instigation, the university began requiring undergraduates to take a political science class, entitled "The Dynamics and Tactics of World Communism."

While Feely took on the communists and fascists, Kinnane's successor, Edward A. Hogan, Jr., took on the radicals in legal education. Thirty-four years old when he took over the deanship, Hogan had been hired by Cassidy in 1935, after finishing his LL.M. at Harvard in the spring of that year. In the flesh, Hogan was gentle and thoughtful, generous and forgiving almost to a fault. On paper, however, in the many essays and law review articles he wrote and published during his twelve years as dean, Hogan was outspoken, almost crusading.

During the year that Hogan was at Harvard, a number of

Dean Edward A. Hogan, Jr. A graduate of Harvard Law School, affable and generous almost to a fault, Hogan was dean from 1939 until 1951. USF ARCHIVES.

law students had attacked the use of the case method of instruction, which had first been developed at Harvard by Dean Christopher C. Langdell in the 1870s. They criticized the law school curriculum for its general lack of integration of the social sciences. Influenced by such writers of the legal realist movement as Karl Llewellyn and Jerome Frank, the students challenged the Langdellian idea that law was an exact science. They maintained, instead, that law emerged out of a relativist cultural context and that there were no specific and universal rights or rules.[2]

For Hogan, and most Catholics, this philosophy was an anathema because it presupposed "the fallacy that man is in fact self-existing and self-sustaining."[3] Hogan believed that the ideas of the legal realists, like those of the Marxists, challenged the beliefs upon which the country had been founded. In an essay published in 1941, he quoted the Declaration of Independence: "... that all men are endowed by their Creator with certain inalienable rights...," and asserted that atheists, agnostics, evolutionists, behaviorists, positivists, and sociological jurists "are at once out of step with the founding fathers."[4]

The launching of the SS Greeley Victory *from Kaiser Shipyards in Oakland. Wartime demand sparked a proliferation of shipyards around the bay, creating jobs and attracting workers from all across the nation.* BANCROFT LIBRARY, HENRY J. KAISER COLLECTION.

IN ANOTHER ARTICLE published in the Spring–Summer 1940 issue of the *San Francisco Quarterly,* the literary journal of the university, Hogan and co-author Edward C. Menager, S.J., claimed that the legal realists, or as they termed them, "the Sociological jurists," were in fact "moving forward with the Marxists." Their aim, according to Hogan and Menager, was "to bring about a maximum of individual self-assertion through a maximum of collective activity." "Unfortunately for them," the authors continued, alluding to the excesses of the Stalin regime, "they must now realize that such a theory produces regimentation in place of liberty."[5]

Hogan elaborated on the ideas implicit in the credo when he wrote an article for the *Georgetown Law Journal* exploring the federal government's role in the resolution of labor disputes and upholding the government's right to regulate labor, as well as capital. He argued that the government should hold employers and employees in balance, sustaining above all the idea of a "living wage." He decried the "super-individualist" philosophy of the day, which he said produced so much industrial discord.[6]

Thus in the early 1940s, at least, the tradition and foundation of what Henry Woods had called "an atmosphere of faith" was still very much a part of legal education at USF. It incorporated a relatively conservative political ideology that, true to its Irish-Catholic roots, was strongly libertarian and highly moral in tone, still deeply committed to the idea of individual civic responsibility, and very much connected to the outlook of the Jesuits and laymen who had founded the school.

Promulgated February 19, 1942, Executive Order 9006 allowed for the removal of 93,000 Japanese-Americans in California for the period of the war. NATIONAL ARCHIVES/ DOROTHEA LANGE.

EVEN BEFORE the Japanese attacked Pearl Harbor, the San Francisco Bay Area had begun preparing for war. Henry Kaiser and his partners had entered into contracts in 1939 to begin building ships under Roosevelt's lend-lease program. The volume of servicemen heading in and out of the Pacific had increased significantly between 1936 and 1940.

After the Japanese attack on Pearl Harbor, however, the social transformations that occurred between 1942 and 1945 were tremendous. More than 1.5 million military personnel passed by or through San Francisco on their way to the Pacific theater. The federal government spent $35 billion on the construction of defense industries and public works in California. As a result, the number of wage earners employed in Bay Area industry rose from 101,000 in 1941 to 269,000 at the peak of wartime production in the spring of 1943. Socially, war-caused hysteria led to the forced relocation of approximately 20,000 people of Japanese descent. Where the Japanese had made their homes—in San Francisco's Fillmore District and Western Addition—immigrant blacks from the South, looking for work in the war industries and victimized by segregated housing policies, moved in by the thousands. San Francisco was, indeed, transformed.[7]

Of all of America's institutions, the colleges and universities were among the hardest hit by the war. Enrollments dropped to a fraction of what they had been, as hundreds of thousands of young men and women went off to fight and to work in the nation's factories. Among law schools, national enrollment dropped from approximately 40,000 to an all-time low of 6,832 in 1943. At USF, enrollment dropped from 114 in 1939 to 51 in 1943.

To accommodate students who were unsure about when they would be inducted into the service, classes were taught in short, intensive nine-week sessions. It was, therefore, possible for a student to take all the required courses in three-fourths of the normal amount of time; during the period of the conflict, the State Bar accepted this accelerated training.

For the first time in the law school's history, women made up a significant portion of each class. In addition, servicemen from various parts of the country stationed in San Francisco took advantage of the special teaching schedule, thus contributing to a further diversification of the student body. Even the physical plant of the university underwent changes during the war years, as temporary buildings were hastily constructed to accommodate several hundred army recruits in training.

By the fall of 1944, the tide had turned in favor of the Allies in both Europe and the Pacific. Victory seemed assured; the price remained uncertain. At home, wartime production had peaked, and even before the surrender of the German and Japanese armies, the production of munitions and weaponry in the United States had begun to decline dramatically.

In 1944, the federal government began to reduce funding for university-related military training. According to USF historian John McGloin, S.J., "The cancellation of student deferments, the induction of eighteen-year-old youths, as well as the phasing out of the ASTP program" reduced USF's enroll-

Law school banquet during World War II. Considerably diminished by the war, the law school survived by attracting a greater percentage of women and catering to the unpredictable schedules of servicemen and men who faced induction. MARVIN CARDOZA.

The war had taken the lives of at least 106 USF students, among them graduates and current students of the law school, including Richard J. Fenton, a first-year student in what should have been the Class of 1943.

ment to 328, cutting revenues by more than 50 percent. That fall, USF was operating at a monthly deficit of more than $6,000. The operation of the law school contributed substantially to that debt, accumulating an aggregate deficit between 1942 and 1946 of $58,810.[8]

Across the nation, some schools faced with similar financial difficulties had closed their professional schools. USF might have done the same except for a substantial fundraising drive spearheaded by Father William Dunne, William H. McCarthy (a longtime Rolph supporter and friend of Matthew Sullivan), Florence McAuliffe (former president of the San Francisco Bar Association), and Daniel Murphy (Crocker Bank executive). Together these men raised nearly $150,000 to cover the school's immediate cash-flow needs.[9]

THEN SUDDENLY the war was over. On August 16, 1945, the day of the Japanese surrender, thousands of people poured onto Market Street wild with relief, anticipation, and jubilation. Servicemen played tug-of-war with fire hoses, sailors grabbed girls in the street, war bonds and bottles were strewn everywhere. Celebration led to riot as the accumulated frustration of the war was vented with abandon. Store windows and street lamps were smashed, and fist fights broke out. It took military and city police two days to control the mob.

The war had taken the lives of at least 106 USF students, among them graduates and current students of the law school, including Richard J. Fenton, a first-year student in what should have been the Class of 1943. At least one faculty member, J. Brent Bodfish, died in action. Henry Howard, a law school graduate of 1946, remembers that of the sixteen men who were in his class before the war, "Only seven survived."[10]

By the fall of 1945, thousands of men every day were being processed out of the service in San Francisco and given a ticket home. Most had been profoundly changed by their experience in the war. The ones who returned to USF returned with a seriousness and sense of purpose unprecedented in the university's past. They were eager to get on with their lives, to start families as well as careers, and the impact of their return was to forever change the nature of legal education at USF.

The end of the war foreshadowed tremendous changes for San Francisco, California, and the nation. Pictured here, a troop ship bringing "the boys" home to San Francisco. SAN FRANCISCO CHRONICLE.

CHAPTER VI

THE SCHOOL TRANSFORMED

ON JUNE 22, 1944, sixteen days after the allies launched their invasion of Europe, President Franklin D. Roosevelt signed the Servicemen's Readjustment Act, otherwise known as the "GI Bill of Rights." Designed to mitigate the sudden influx of workers into the labor pool in the aftermath of the war and to acknowledge the services rendered by American military personnel, the GI Bill entitled veterans to unemployment insurance for a year, guaranteed loans for building homes or establishing businesses, and, most significantly for the nation's universities and professional schools, provided money to cover educational expenses.

As early as the fall of 1945, USF felt the impact of the returning GIs—law school enrollment increased to 109, more than twice the 1943 total. The trickle, however, turned to a flood by 1947, when there were 357 students enrolled. And by 1948, when there were 450, the school had reached absolute capacity.

Parade followed parade as troops from the Pacific theater came home via San Francisco. Thanks to the GI Bill of Rights, every vet was entitled to educational benefits, resulting in an enrollment explosion across the country. SAN FRANCISCO CHRONICLE.

Evidencing the tremendous change in the character of the law school student body, 89 percent of the students received veterans' educational benefits, more than 65 percent were over the age of twenty-five, approximately 55 percent were married, and only 57 percent were Roman Catholic. Nevertheless, despite the huge social dislocations caused by the war, 40 percent of the students were graduates or former students of USF, and the vast majority were natives of the Bay Area.[1]

With this tremendous growth in the student population, the third floor of Campion Hall was crowded, to say the least. The law library, separated from the main university library by a set of swinging doors, could accommodate only sixty-eight students at a time. Classes had to be held in the temporary buildings constructed in 1943 for the ASTP program.

THE END OF THE WAR caught most of the state's law schools inadequately prepared for the tremendous influx of students. Ten years of Depression, combined with increasingly restrictive admission standards, and then the war, had put six of the state's twenty-one schools out of business. Most of those that had managed to keep their doors open had done so by cutting faculty, deferring building maintenance and construction, and seeking outright subsidy.

The chaos that resulted from such a sudden change of circumstances caused anxiety in a number of corners. Within the State Bar, some practitioners became concerned about the impact of a predicted 33 percent increase in the number of lawyers in the state by the end of the decade. There was also some concern that the quality of legal education would suffer as a result of overcrowding. The ever-present advocates of increased standards and more restrictive admissions took advantage of the climate to press for higher standards for law students, law schools, and bar applicants.

In response to these challenges, the State Bar created a Special Survey Board, similar to the Survey Committee of 1933, and authorized it to assess the status of legal education in the state and to determine what, if any, changes should be made. Composed of three outstanding legal scholars from outside the state—Joseph A. McClain, Jr., Thomas F. McDonald, and Sidney Post Simpson—the board visited each of the state's fifteen law schools in the early months of 1949 and submitted its preliminary findings to each school in June.

Before the board's recommendations were made public, the fallout from the evaluation process itself was significant. Early in 1949, during the course of an on-site inspection, Survey Director Sidney Post Simpson had suggested to Father President Dunne that Dean Edward Hogan should be replaced. For a number of years, Hogan had suffered from a rheumatic heart condition that made it difficult for him to climb stairs; he had to have an office on the first floor of Campion, which removed him from the rest of the law school. Simpson suggested that "in view of Dean Hogan's health, it is unfair to himself and his family... that he be continued in an administrative position."[2]

Father President Dunne took Simpson's recommendation to heart. Early in the spring of 1949—before the report of the survey board had been published and long before he said anything to Hogan—Dunne and Raymond Feely, then dean of

The composition of the law school student population changed dramatically after the war. Eighty percent of the new students received some form of veterans' benefits. In contrast to earlier generations of law students, many of the returning vets were already raising families, as shown in this 1948 Christmas party photograph. EDWARD T. TAYLOR, JR.

faculties, began to look around for a new dean of the law school. Dunne asked Florence McAuliffe, among others, to make inquiries, and by June he seemed to have decided on Vernon X. Miller, dean of Loyola University School of Law in New Orleans. That summer, Dunne met with Miller in San Francisco and for all intents and purposes offered him the job at USF beginning in the fall of 1950. Miller tacitly accepted, contingent upon Dunne's ability to work out the details.[3]

In December of 1949, Father President William Dunne wrote a note to Hogan, reminding him of Simpson's recommendation and stating that, after six months of searching, he believed he had found a possible candidate at Loyola University in New Orleans. Dunne suggested that Hogan become dean emeritus and otherwise continue to teach; at the end of his letter, he wrote, "Your health is the entire point in the matter."[4]

Hogan, however, did not want to give up the deanship. He suggested instead that the school hire an associate or vice-dean who would handle day-to-day internal affairs while the dean would be responsible for external relations, curriculum, and the budget, as well as his own scholarship.[5]

Dunne now found himself in an awkward position. He had already begun to negotiate with Miller and correctly anticipated that Miller would not accept a "step down" to come to USF; nevertheless, it seems clear that he felt he could work things out with Hogan, because on January 5, 1950, he made Miller an offer.

The whole affair blew up when Miller unwittingly wrote to Hogan, assuming that Hogan had agreed to the deal, and asked him to poll the faculty to find out whether they would accept him as dean. Hogan did poll the faculty, but on the question of hiring Miller as associate or assistant dean. He then telegrammed Miller that the faculty was in favor of such an arrangement.

Upon realizing that Hogan had not accepted Dunne's offer to become dean emeritus, that in fact he was tenaciously holding to his position, Miller telegrammed Dunne, saying ". . . under the circumstances, I cannot accept your offer." Later, he wrote to Dunne: "The situation is unfortunate but I can understand why Dean Hogan thinks he should have been consulted about his successor. I would have felt that way too, were I in his position."[6]

In the wake of this fiasco over the deanship, the spring of 1950 was a difficult time for the law school. Although Hogan continued as dean, and no further move was made to replace him, Father President Dunne and at least some of the faculty expected that, in view of all that had happened, Hogan would announce his resignation on the last day of classes.

The publication of the Simpson Report caused a full review of the school by a committee of faculty, alumni, and university administration. The Special Survey Board had noted a continued "undue reliance on part-time teachers, particularly in the night division." And although it determined that the pay scale for part-timers was adequate, the board pointed out that "the salary scale for full-time teachers is not such as will attract and keep men of superior ability."[7]

The Class of 1949 on the steps outside Campion Hall. Pictured at bottom are faculty members. From left to right: William Q. deFuniak, E.L. Merica, Charles P. Knights, Edward A. Hogan, and C.F. Stanley. Librarian Elizabeth Anne Quigley stands just behind Merica and Knights. USF ARCHIVES.

The groundbreaking for Gleeson Library. In 1949, Father William J. Dunne launched a major building program on Ignatian Heights, which lasted through the fifties and sixties. Finished in 1950, Gleeson Library was the centerpiece of the first phase of that campaign. USF ARCHIVES.

Shedding some light on the pragmatic nature of most of the students, the board noted that "subjects not included in the bar examination are not popular with the students; the course in International Law, for example, has never had over five students." Overall, however, the board suggested that "if given a decent physical plant and adequate financial support," the school could be developed into a "first-rate law school."[8]

The Special Survey Board had described USF's physical plant as "by far the most inadequate of any American Bar Association-approved school in California." But if USF was the worst, it was certainly not alone. Hastings was "extremely overcrowded," the facilities at Stanford were "inadequate in all respects," and the situation at Boalt was worse than it was in 1933 when the California Survey Committee had described Boalt Memorial Hall of Law as a "beautiful building... but crowded to an extreme degree."[9]

At USF, overcrowding was apparent all over campus and was as frustrating to Father President Dunne as it was to the students and faculty of the law school. Disappointed by the lack of progress on building construction, Dunne had written a letter in February of 1946 addressed to Father Provincial Joseph King, stating, "After nearly eight years here I am beginning to understand why we are so often regarded as a 'Junior College' or even, by some, as an 'overgrown high school.'"[10]

Dunne's strategy for expansion and for enhancing the prestige of the institution centered on the creation of a university board of regents, whose first and primary task was to organize the university's "Greater USF Fund." The goal of the campaign was to raise money to finance the construction of a number of buildings, including a new library, a gymnasium, a science building, faculty residence, and a law school.

A new university library was the first building on Dunne's list, and in May of 1949, even before the fund drive was launched, ground was broken for the construction of Gleeson Hall, with completion expected sometime in the summer of 1950. The original plans did not include housing the law school, but with the publication of the report of the State Bar Special Survey Board, the university was forced to find more space for the school immediately or risk losing ABA approval and state accreditation. Accordingly, Dunne announced that the law school would take over the third floor of the library as "temporary" quarters until a law building could be constructed.

In the fall of 1950, the law school moved to Gleeson. Students packed the books in the law library, vacuuming and sorting each one as they went. A moving company lowered the

ELIZABETH ANNE QUIGLEY

RICHARD CHATCUFF

When she came to USF in September of 1946, there were fourteen thousand volumes in the law school's library. When she retired from her position as head law librarian in 1983, the collection had multiplied ten times over.

Elizabeth Anne Quigley grew up in Minnesota and took a B.A. in English and Library Sciences from the College of St. Catherine's in St. Paul. She came to San Francisco shortly before the outbreak of World War II to work at the San Francisco College of Women (Lone Mountain) and came to USF at the height of the G.I. Bill boom.

Anne Quigley oversaw the library's growth and its relocation from Campion Hall to Gleeson Library in 1950, and then from Gleeson to Kendrick Hall in 1962. She worked closely with the faculty and nine different deans and acting deans to maintain the law school's compliance with the standards of the ABA and the AALS.

Despite the conditions, Quigley remembers with fondness her early years at USF. "I felt closer when we were all crowded together in Gleeson," she says. "I had more contact with the students." By the time she retired, after thirty-seven years with the school, Quigley had seen more students come and go than any other member of the faculty.

boxes down from the third floor with a winch, and students formed a human chain to pass boxes across campus. The process took two and a half days, and when it was over, Law Librarian Anne Quigley threw a party for all the students who had helped. Father President Dunne predicted that the school would be housed in Gleeson for not more than ten years. He was almost right.

Throughout 1950, things around the law school seemed to go from bad to worse. The school's bar pass rate, which had averaged over 80 percent for two years, had fallen to 61.9 percent in the fall of 1949, and fell to 53.3 percent in the spring. For yet another reason, the school was concerned about losing its accreditation.

Since accreditation had begun in 1937, the State Bar had implemented what had come to be called "the accreditation rule," whereby a school was expected to maintain a certain standard of success on the bar. That standard started at 30 percent in 1937, rose to 45 percent in 1942, climbed to 50

Concern about the dramatic increase in lawyers following the postwar boom prompted the San Francisco Examiner *to run this photo of the spring 1949 bar exam with the headline: "Too Many Lawyers Now, and More Graduating."* SAN FRANCISCO EXAMINER.

percent in 1947, and peaked at 60 percent in 1949. Among faculty and administrators in the less elite or more "democratic" schools, there was a strong suspicion that the State Bar was trying to force out a number of law schools and thereby reduce the number of candidates attempting the bar. Outspoken critics of the accreditation rule, including Dean Hogan and Dean David Snodgrass of Hastings, argued that the rule placed undue emphasis on the bar examination and that it wrongfully charged against schools students who had flunked or not graduated.[11]

Tensions had been building around this issue since before the war, but in July of 1950, precipitated in part by the Special Survey Board's criticism of the rule, the issue came to a head at a public meeting of the Committee of Bar Examiners held in San Francisco. Dean Hogan argued on behalf of a number of schools for accreditation based primarily on ABA approval and generally on the maintenance of certain standards of educational policy and not based on the results of the bar.

As a result of that meeting, the Committee of Bar Examiners began to concede their position slightly. In November of 1950, the State Bar decided to allow a grace period for any school that fell below the 60 percent pass-rate figure. During this grace period, the school would remain accredited, pending a full investigation conducted by the bar examiners. In 1952, the State Bar retreated completely and accepted a rule—substantially the same as that proposed by Snodgrass, Hogan, and others—that abolished the pass-rate requirement and paralleled the ABA in assessing educational policy first.

The revision of the accreditation rule came just in time for USF, as the three-year pass rate dipped below 60 percent in the fall of 1952. The outcome of the struggle, however, was also significant for the deanship, as Hogan formed a close bond with David Snodgrass at Hastings.

In the fall of 1950, the university administration began to relieve Hogan of his responsibilities, appointing A. Russell Berti to the position of associate dean, informing Hogan that at the end of the year he would be relieved of his position entirely, and once again offering him the title of dean emeritus.

Dunne went back to Vernon Miller, and Miller accepted Dunne's offer to start as dean in the fall of 1951. The whole matter came out in the newspapers in December, and in January, Hogan accepted Snodgrass' offer to come to Hastings. Russell Berti was appointed acting dean for the remainder of the year, and in February Hogan left USF after fifteen years on the faculty.

San Francisco celebrated the centennial anniversary of "the city's university" in 1955. Newspaper feature stories acknowledged the important part USF had played in developing much of the city's leadership, and they anticipated the school's significant role in shaping the city's future. USF ARCHIVES/HAAS & ASSOCIATES.

CHAPTER VII

A TIME TO REBUILD

THE SCHOOL VERNON X. MILLER inherited in the fall of 1951 had been shaken considerably by the roller coaster years of the GI boom, the accreditation battles, and the unfortunate end of the Hogan affair. In the spring of 1951, the bar pass rate fell to 41.3 percent as twenty-seven of forty-six first-time takers failed the test. That fall, the results were even worse: thirty-six out of fifty-eight flunked, a pass rate of only 37.9 percent.

Miller was hired to implement serious reforms within the law school. His reputation within the community of legal educators was outstanding. A member of the Executive Committee of the Association of American Law Schools, a graduate of the University of Minnesota with a J.D. from Yale, Miller had taught law since 1926 and had been dean at Loyola University, New Orleans, for almost eleven years. In addition, according to the dean of the Fordham University School of Law who had recommended him, Miller was "Catholic beyond any doubt."[1]

John Edward Benson, Jr., on graduation day in 1955 with six-month-old twin daughters, Elaine and Evelyn, son John Edward Benson III (left), age two, and daughter Kathleen (right), age four. JOHN EDWARD BENSON, JR.

Dean Vernon X. Miller and Father Francis Callahan with a student. Following Raymond Feely's heart attack, Callahan played an increasingly important part in law school affairs, first as regent and later as the university's development officer. USF ARCHIVES/HAAS & ASSOCIATES.

When he took the job, Miller understood that he could not make dramatic changes overnight. Hogan had been a very popular man with a reputation for leniency and tolerance. After twelve years of his administration, a certain amount of inconsistency in the application of standards and in grading had become apparent among the faculty and within admissions. In fact, evidence suggests that Hogan had admitted students who had been failed by other law schools and acquiesced when students who were flunked out of USF came to him asking to be reinstated.

IN JANUARY, Miller circulated a memorandum to the faculty, noting the dismal results of the fall bar exam, concluding, "I think it is a fair deduction . . . that we give too many high grades and pass too many people." To make some effort to impose a grading standard, Miller announced, "If any instructor gives premium grades of 'A' or 'B' to more than 20% of the students enrolled in any class, no grades will be entered for the students in that course until the instructor has discussed his questions and his papers with me."[2]

This directive did not go over well, however. When grades for the fall semester were turned in, two professors failed to observe the 20 percent rule. After consultation with Miller, one professor agreed to revise his grades; the other, Clinton F. Stanley, took his case to his students and eventually to the newspapers. The incident turned into a minor scandal, and eventually Stanley was fired. Both Miller and Feely, who was academic vice-president at the time, were embarrassed.

In the aftermath of the incident, however, Miller's relationship with Feely began to sour. That summer, after the spring bar results were published and USF was once again at the bottom of the list of ABA-approved schools, the two got into a bitter feud. Feely argued that drastic steps needed to be taken immediately, that the school's reputation would not sustain any more bad news. Miller argued that fairness dictated that higher standards be phased in gradually and that the school must simply bite the bullet until a transition could be made.

Both Miller and Feely blamed the poor bar results on Hogan's relaxation of the standards for admission, and both admitted that the school's poor results on the bar would continue until those weaker students who had been admitted by Hogan were out of the system. With a stricter grading standard in place, Feely favored flunking any senior who did not maintain a C average throughout the final year, and he threatened to impose such a rule even over Miller's objection. Feely's concern was for improving the school's bar pass rate immediately.

Miller argued that it would be unfair to change the rules of the game so dramatically after a student had been admitted and carried and had paid his tuition for so long. He pointed out that no other California school applied such a standard and that it was the responsibility of the school to exclude unqualified students well before the senior year. A compromise was implemented that fall whereby students would be graduated with a C average minus three points.

Miller argued that it would be unfair to change the rules of the game so dramatically after a student had been admitted and carried and had paid his tuition for so long.

Despite his efforts to be fair, however, Miller bore the brunt of student reaction to the tougher standards. A committee organized in the spring of 1953 accused the dean of "scholastic robbery." In a letter to Father President William Dunne, the students charged that Miller had dropped a number of professors' grades and that students who had previously been on the honor roll were now getting Cs. About their grades, they asserted, "When we earn them they are ours, and he who steals them is a thief, just as surely had he stolen bread from our tables; and just as surely again, it will be our families and our children who will go hungry. If it is the bar average he is endeavoring to raise, there must be a more honorable and decent method."[3]

By the summer of 1953, Miller had had enough. His relationship with Feely had gone from bad to worse. At the outset of the 1953–1954 academic year, the last year of Miller's three-year contract, memoranda between the two were caustic at best. Feely asserted that he and Father President Dunne had been misled about Miller; Miller found that hard to swallow since both had worked on his appointment for almost two years.

Despite the fact that bar results had shown steady improvement, averaging over 61 percent between the fall of 1952 and the spring–fall of 1953, Feely continued to take issue with Miller's policies, reminding him, as he had reminded Lewis Cassidy and other law school deans before, that "I am a graduate of our Law School, have been a teaching member of the Law Faculty in several fields and, at one time, was Regent of the Law School."[4]

Miller's attitude, for the most part, was one of disappointment and frustration. In a letter to Father President Dunne, he wrote: "I can tell you that we have too many bosses for a school

Possibly taken on the occasion of Vernon X. Miller's arrival at USF, this photo includes (facing forward): Rev. Francis Callahan, Dean Vernon X. Miller, and Father William J. Dunne. Standing to the left: Francis R. Walsh and A. Russell Berti. USF ARCHIVES/ HAAS & ASSOCIATES.

of our size."[5] Later, he frankly confessed that he was looking for other work. Father President Dunne, attempting to mitigate Feely's influence, offered to extend Miller's contract, but Miller declined. "You have been generous to me ever since I have been here," he wrote, "and I would not want to leave if I were sure you and I could work together year after year. I know that your tenure is limited, and that has been a factor in helping me decide what I should do."[6] Dunne regretfully accepted Miller's decision.

In the spring of 1954, when he was offered the deanship at Columbus School of Law at Catholic University, Miller accepted the position. He remained at Columbus for seventeen years, serving as president of the AALS in 1965, and from 1970 to 1973, he was a member of the Council of the Section on Legal Education of the ABA.

In 1978, in a letter to Preston Devine, Miller described his tenure at USF as a "housekeeping job," and indeed it was. Despite Feely's criticisms, Miller managed to strengthen the program at USF considerably. In 1955, the year immediately following Miller's resignation, when the first class of graduates who had spent their entire law-school career under his deanship applied to become lawyers, thirty-one of thirty-four candidates passed the test for an overall score of 91 percent, the highest overall pass rate the school's graduates had achieved since the exam was revised in 1928. In fact, over the next three years, as students who had been admitted under Miller continued to graduate, the school maintained a three-year average pass rate of almost 82 percent and consistently ranked among the state's top schools.

In the wake of Miller's resignation, the university administration promoted A. Russell Berti from associate dean to acting dean. If a search for a new dean was begun immediately, it was probably sidetracked in the fall by the transfer of Father President William Dunne and the appointment of a new president, Father John F.X. Connolly, S.J.

The Gleeson librarians, including Law School Librarian Elizabeth Anne Quigley (third from the left). The School of Law occupied the third floor of Gleeson from 1950 until 1962. USF ARCHIVES.

USF students demonstrating outside City Hall following the Soviet invasion of Hungary in 1956. MONITOR FILES, ARCHIVES OF THE ARCHDIOCESE/RAY DEARAGON.

In his book, *Jesuits by the Golden Gate,* historian John McGloin suggests that Father John Connolly's assumption of the presidency was not necessarily easy. Connolly had been assigned to the community before, but his previous work had not involved the university. He was clearly committed to continuing Father Dunne's expansion program, but was distracted early on by the need to begin planning the celebration of the university's centennial scheduled for the 1955–1956 academic year.[7]

WITH RUSSELL BERTI as acting dean, the situation at the law school was clearly not critical. Berti was a St. Ignatius product who had started in the high school in 1918, graduated from the college in 1926, and received his LL.B. from the law school in 1928. He had taught at the university, both in the English department and the law school, for almost twenty-five years.

As a teacher in the undergraduate program, Berti had founded the St. Ives Law Club in 1934 for students interested in pursuing a legal career. Many of the men who graduated from the law school in the late thirties and forties had been members. In fact, Berti had either been in school with or taught almost every law school graduate between the years of 1924 and 1955. In that sense, he was as much a part of the institution as Raymond Feely himself.

During Dean Hogan's periods of illness, Berti and Margaret Proctor, the law school's registrar and secretary since the late 1920s, had run the school and kept all the pieces together. In September of 1950, Berti was named associate dean under Hogan with practical responsibility for all the internal and day-to-day operations of the school. When Hogan left for Hastings in January of 1951, Berti finished out the school year as acting dean.

Berti thus was more than able to serve as caretaker of the law school until a permanent dean could be found. Indeed, as the graduates of the Miller years began to take the bar and as the school's average soared in the spring and fall of 1955, the administration apparently felt quite comfortable postponing any decision.

The year 1955 was a golden year in more ways than one for the community of students, faculty, administration, and alumni who made up the University of San Francisco. In

A. RUSSELL BERTI

KEN McLAUGHLIN

During the course of a career that spanned fifty-three years at USF, A. Russell Berti was called upon on three different occasions by the Jesuits of St. Ignatius to take over the law school. As Berti himself says, "I outlasted them all."

He was the quintessential St. Ignatius student—born of Irish and Italian stock, a second-generation San Franciscan. He grew up playing sandlot baseball and handball with kids who would later be fellow USF law school grads—Raymond Sullivan, Melvin Cronin, and Vincent Hallinan among them. When he was ready for high school, Berti says, "I thought I was going to Lowell, but my father had other ideas." Instead, Berti started at St. Ignatius in 1918.

From 1918 to 1971, when he retired from his position as professor of law at USF, Berti was almost constantly connected with St. Ignatius and USF. After high school, he started college at "the shirt factory," and when he was a junior in college, he started going to law school at the same time. The year he graduated from the law school, he enrolled at U.C. Berkeley and took a masters degree in English. Even while he was studying in Berkeley, he began teaching English in the college at St. Ignatius.

Berti began "helping out" in the law school in 1935 and became permanently affiliated with the school in 1939. Off and on in the late forties and early fifties, Berti would take over many of the dean's responsibilities when Ed Hogan was sick. Gradually, Berti assumed more and more of the dean's ongoing responsibilities, and, in 1950, Father President Dunne appointed him associate dean under Hogan.

"The idea was that Hogan would handle outside affairs and I would run the law school," Berti says, "but Feely and Hogan did not get along and it was just a matter of time. We were at the Edgewater Beach Hotel in Chicago that Christmas for a convention and Hogan told me he was going to resign." When Hogan left USF for Hastings, Berti became acting dean and continued in the position until Vernon Miller was hired and began work the next fall.

Three years later, when Miller left for Catholic University, Berti once again became acting dean. This time his tenure lasted almost three years. He instituted bar-review courses and emphasized a more practical third-year curriculum. When Frank Walsh was hired in 1957, Berti returned to teaching and his own law practice.

Finally, in 1970, after Frank Walsh left to take a position at the Federal Communications Commission and acting dean William Riegger moved over to Hastings, Russell Berti became dean again. The cover of the *Forum* had a picture of him wearing dark sunglasses and riding a burro. It somehow captured Berti's sense of humor and his tenacity.

Faced with a changing and almost volatile student body, Berti worked to improve relations among faculty members, and between faculty and students and alumni and faculty. Berti wrote a regular column for the newly inaugurated *Forum* and attempted to be candid and honest about the law school. He instituted a commission to study curriculum reform and enhanced the clinical program. In 1972, after a year's sabbatical in Africa, Berti retired.

Bill Russell, star of the 1955 and 1956 USF basketball team, which won two national championships. USF ARCHIVES.

March, the Dons captured the first of two successive NCAA titles in basketball. This success fueled the fundraising drive for a new gymnasium, which, in general, enhanced the feeling that the university was in an expansionist mode.

Centennial activities continued through the spring of 1956, and it was not until the fall that the university administration had the opportunity to turn to the selection of a new dean for the law school. Shortly after the start of the new academic year, Father Raymond Feely had a serious heart attack; in his place, Father Francis Callahan, S.J., emerged as the principal advisor to the president on matters pertaining to the law school.

Callahan and Connolly were apparently intent on finding someone who would build the image of the law school. While they thought highly of Russell Berti, it was obvious that they needed someone who was not a graduate of the institution, who nevertheless had some affinity for the school, who could enforce the standards initiated by Miller, and who had a reputation in his own right that would benefit the school.

The man they selected fit almost all their criteria and was representative of the new generation of lawyers who had come of age during the war. A naval officer in the Pacific during World War II, Francis R. Walsh had come home in 1945 to a new wife, a baby boy, and law school at Georgetown. When he graduated in 1948, he was near the top of his class.

Walsh and his wife had both fallen in love with San Francisco during the war and had decided to return at the first opportunity. That opportunity presented itself in 1949 when Judge William Healy of the Ninth Circuit Court of Appeals offered Walsh a clerkship. The next year, Walsh returned to Georgetown to teach, but came back to San Francisco in 1951 to join the faculty at USF.

When he became dean of the law school at thirty-three, Walsh was the youngest law dean in the country. In 1952, *Time* magazine had recognized him as one of "San Francisco's 100 Newsmakers of Tomorrow." He had served as president of the Barristers Club of San Francisco. He had spent almost three years in private practice with the firm of Wallace & Parker and, during that time, had developed a solid reputation among the members of the bar of San Francisco.

In short, Walsh was an ambitious and affable man on the rise, and Connolly and Callahan were pleased to get him. They were already laying out the strategy for the university's "Second Century" expansion, and Walsh would prove to be a valuable part of that strategy's implementation.

Ignatian Heights at the end of the 1950s. USF ARCHIVES/ VANO WELLS FAGLIANO.

CHAPTER VIII

FIFTY YEARS AND A HOME

IN 1951, WHEN THE LAW SCHOOL moved into Gleeson Library, Father President Dunne said that he expected the school to have its own building within ten years. With the conclusion of the centennial and the hiring of a new dean for the law school, Father President Connolly and Father Callahan now turned to making Dunne's prophecy a reality.

USF at the end of the 1950s was teetering on the precipice of a new era in higher education. Expansion of the University of California system had already begun in the late forties with the upgrading of facilities at Santa Barbara, Davis, and Riverside. A master plan in the works called for the addition of new campuses at Santa Cruz, Irvine, and San Diego. Locally, state colleges in San Francisco, Hayward, and San Jose were improved. These expansions of opportunity for public higher education directly threatened USF's potential enrollment, particularly if the university's increasingly outdated facilities made it more and more difficult for the school to compete.

Ground was broken for Kendrick Hall on May 23, 1961. Posed together for the occasion are Father President John Connolly, Charles Kendrick, and Dean Francis R. Walsh. USF ARCHIVES/VANO PHOTOGRAPHY.

... the USF administration in 1959 began to put in place its most ambitious fundraising drive to date, one that would, in the end, dramatically transform both the school and the nature of its administration.

The situation for the law school was not much better. Demand for legal education slowly increased throughout the fifties, but new facilities at UCLA, Boalt, and Hastings allowed those schools to siphon off most of the excess in student population. Indeed, between 1953, when Hastings dedicated its new building on McAllister Street, and 1964, Hastings enrollments rose steadily from just under 400 to almost 1,100.[1]

Understanding that new construction on Ignatian Heights was of paramount importance to the school's viability in its second century, the USF administration in 1959 began to put in place its most ambitious fundraising drive to date, one that would, in the end, dramatically transform both the school and the nature of its administration. With the help of PG&E President James Black, Connolly and Callahan assembled a President's Council of Advisors that included some of the most influential men in San Francisco, among them the Honorable Preston Devine, a graduate of the law school; Jerd F. Sullivan, Jr., president of Crocker Bank and son of Jeremiah Sullivan, and Charles Kendrick, president of Schlage Lock Company.

ON MAY 1, 1959, the council met for the first time. Father President Connolly outlined the council's purpose, and the members elected Kendrick chairman. Over the course of the next year, the council met frequently, working with Callahan (who had been appointed director of development), to develop priorities for building and a strategy for raising an estimated $3 million. In the process, the university, with the council's approval, hired architect Milton Pflueger to draw up plans for a new science center and a new law school building.

Pflueger and Dean Walsh met frequently in the winter and spring of 1960, and Pflueger came back with three alternate designs: two fairly conventional, the other an innovative nautilus concept. Walsh picked the nautilus. According to Walsh, "Kendrick was concerned about the design. At a president's council meeting he interrogated me like a lawyer, asking me why I wanted it round. Suddenly Charles Harney, who was a contractor, piped up and said, 'Charlie, did you ever see a round gas tank?' Kendrick nodded his head at that point and then we went on. From that point on no one questioned the design."[2]

Pflueger's designs, coupled with the growing realization

that the university would need additional money for programmatic expansions, quickly raised the overall price tag on the campaign to $5.5 million, a figure that concerned a number of council members, especially Charles Kendrick. That spring the university, with the council's approval, hired Thomas Jordan, an experienced fundraiser from the University of St. Louis, to direct the campaign.

According to Jordan, the council was concerned because a similar campaign for Grace Cathedral was faltering and would be lucky, it appeared, to raise even a million dollars. "I pointed out that the largest gift to date from the organizers of that campaign was only $50,000," said Jordan. "The first major gift is always the most important; it sets the pace."[3]

The President's Advisory Council. From left to right: Francis J. Callahan, S.J.; Edmund J. Smyth, S.J.; Mortimer J. Fleishhacker, Jr.; Thomas J. Mellon; Harry Bardt; Marco Hellman; Charles W. Dullea, S.J.; Charles Kendrick; Edward Littlefield; Preston Devine; Jerd Sullivan; Jack How; Lyell McLaren; Roger Lapham, Jr.; and Thomas F. Jordan. VANO WELLS FAGLIANO.

CHARLES H. KENDRICK

MOULIN STUDIOS

Charles Kendrick's donation of $1 million in 1960 toward the construction of a new School of Law for the University of San Francisco is considered by some to have been the single most important contribution in the school's history. It assured the success of the university's "Second Century" campaign and propelled the physical expansion of the university at a critical time in the school's history.

Although he was admitted to the California bar in 1902, Kendrick never practiced. Instead, he began his career in real estate, selling property in Petaluma and the North Bay, investing in land in San Francisco both before and after the earthquake. As a businessman, Kendrick made his mark principally in the twenties and thirties by developing two fledgling enterprises—S.O.S. (steel wool & soap) and Schlage Lock—into multimillion-dollar companies.

He was, indeed, a patron of USF and of the city of San Francisco in a fashion that was characteristic of his era and is now all but forgotten. As chairman of the Committee To Build a San Francisco War Memorial, he oversaw the construction of the War Memorial Opera House and the Veterans Building, which were completed in 1932. He served on the Mayor's Emergency Relief Committee during the Depression, was later chairman of the Board of Trustees of Mills College, and vice-president of the California School of Fine Arts. He was considered one of "the Big Five" among San Francisco's men of public life.

In 1959, when James Black began working with Fathers Callahan and Connolly to organize the President's Council of Advisors, Kendrick was eighty-three years old. He was drawn to USF's needs for several reasons—first among these was his love for San Francisco and his perception that USF had been, and should continue to be, the city's university. He was genuinely impressed with the accomplishments of the university's graduates and with the university's collective contribution to the city.

As chairman of the Council of Advisors, Kendrick developed a deep respect for Father President John Connolly. Near the end of his life, Kendrick also became enamored of the Jesuit perspective, of their teaching, and of their commitment to values he shared. His sympathy for the needs of the law school was born of his own apprenticeship before the bar, but was especially rooted in the tragic death of his son, Charles F. Kendrick, a Marine fighter pilot who was killed in action over Guadalcanal in 1942.

At twenty-five, Kendrick's son had been an outstanding scholar, a student at Harvard Law before he enlisted in the navy, and a decorated combatant before he was shot down. Two years after the fighting ceased, Kendrick had gone to Guadalcanal to personally search through the war-torn jungles in hopes of finding his son's hastily covered grave. Miraculously, he found it and brought the boy's remains home to San Francisco.

Following the completion and the dedication of Kendrick Hall, Kendrick continued to take an active interest in the development of the university and the law school. When a casual observer commented in Kendrick's presence on the rows of empty shelves in the new library, Kendrick became concerned and afterwards donated another $250,000 over the next five years to spend on book acquisitions. He also donated $250,000 for law scholarships. Recognizing Charles and Kathryn Kendrick's generosity, the university conferred upon them the title "Founders of the University."

Kendrick had already planned to give $50,000 to help launch the "Second Century" project, but early in the spring of 1960, he called Father President John Connolly to say that he knew a man willing to give a million dollars to assure the construction of the law school and to propel the fundraising campaign to a higher level; that man turned out to be Kendrick himself.

In October, Connolly announced Kendrick's donation to the world: "Great deeds demand great individuals; at a time of exceptional need, it is most heartening to find individuals such as Mr. and Mrs. Kendrick . . . we will always consider their gift a turning point upward in our history."[4] In retrospect, Tom Jordan described Kendrick's gift as the "single most important gift in the school's history because it set the pace for giving in that campaign."[5]

Kendrick Hall under construction. In the spring of 1962, work was slowed by a strike that shut down construction projects throughout the state. Nevertheless, work was completed in time for the law school's fiftieth anniversary. USF ARCHIVES/VANO WELLS FAGLIANO.

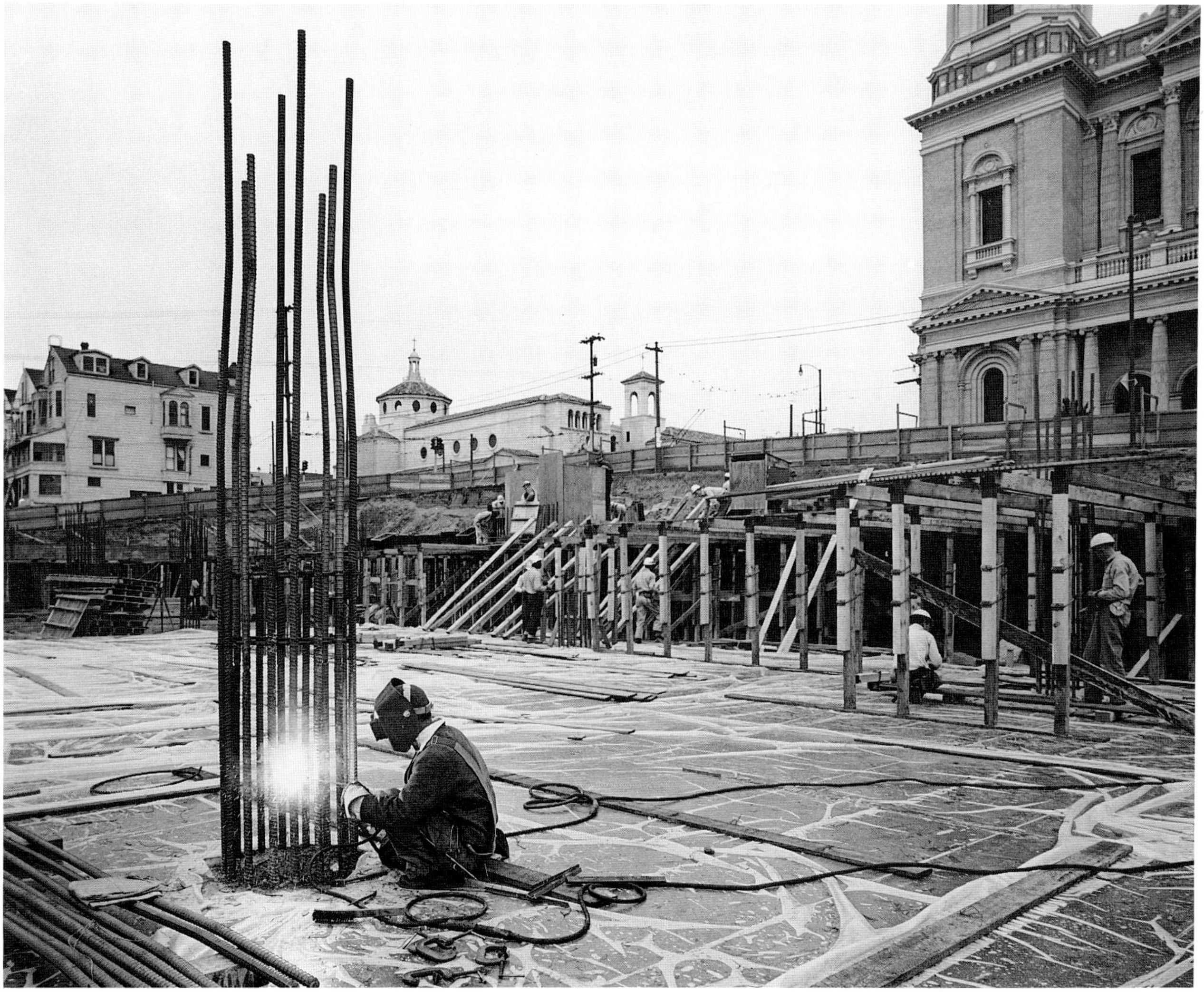

Groundbreaking for Kendrick Hall took place on May 23, 1961, with Father President Connolly and Mr. and Mrs. Kendrick posing for cameras, hands joined on the wooden handle of a shovel. In the spring of 1962, progress was slowed by a statewide strike that shut down construction jobs throughout the state. But by September of 1962, in time for the fiftieth anniversary of the opening of the school, the new building was ready for occupation.

The weekend of September 28, 1962, was a whirlwind of celebration, commemoration, and congratulation. Friday afternoon, a convocation was held in Campion Hall at which three former law professors—Joseph Farry, William A. Breen, and James E. Burns—were honored for their long years of service. That night the Law Society held its own dinner and celebration. The next morning, Kendrick Hall was dedicated and blessed by Archbishop Joseph T. McGucken, and Herman Phleger gave the keynote address. The ceremonies culminated Saturday night in the Grand Ballroom of the Fairmont Hotel, where

Dean Francis Walsh speaking at the dedication of Kendrick Hall. USF ARCHIVES/VANO WELLS FAGLIANO.

almost 1,200 people gathered to hear a speech by Robert F. Kennedy, then attorney general of the United States.

Anniversaries and dedications give rise to retrospectives and prognostications; they also offer a snapshot of an institution taken in a single moment, caught between its past and its future. The speeches delivered on the occasion of the school's fiftieth anniversary offer profound insight into the times and the nature of the USF School of Law at the beginning of the 1960s.

Scheduled to be the featured speaker at the Kendrick Hall dedication dinner, Attorney General Robert F. Kennedy had to cancel his appearance when racial tensions at the University of Mississippi threatened to erupt into violence. Kennedy nevertheless delivered his speech to the assembled crowd by means of a special telephone hookup. Sometime later, he visited USF and spoke to the assembled student body. USF ARCHIVES/VANO PHOTOGRAPHY.

BY 1962, USF was apparently like almost any other law school in the country. It could claim its distinguished and accomplished graduates. Alumni, faculty, and students could point with pride to the school's recent record on the bar. What distinguished the school as a Jesuit law school, however, as a place where "the atmosphere of faith" was as important as the quality of professional education, was more elusive and must be understood within the context of the state of legal education in the early sixties.

By the end of the 1950s, the American Bar Association and the Association of American Law Schools had accomplished virtually everything they had set out to do at the turn of the century with regard to legal education. Standards had been established and adopted by law schools, state bar associations, and legislatures across the country. Unaccredited schools had either been driven out of business or forced to come up to standard. By 1958, out of a total of 42,646 students enrolled in law school, more than 92 percent were in ABA-approved schools, compared to less than 83 percent in 1949 and only 32.2 percent in 1928. Three years of college before law school had become the norm. Even more significantly, by the middle 1950s, the number of lawyers who had been to college finally exceeded the number of lawyers who hadn't.[6]

The general effect of all this homogenization was to make it increasingly difficult to distinguish the elite schools from the nonelite. According to Robert Stevens, "The triumph of the AALS was to prove the triumph of the good second-level schools at the expense of the elitist institutions."[7] USF was certainly a good example in this regard. The school's three-year average on the bar for the years 1955 through 1957 rose to almost 82 percent, among the best in the state. In the spring of 1957, the school's moot court team defeated Hastings and

Stanford in regional competition and went on to place fourth in the nation.

But as the number of law schools approved by the ABA and the AALS increased, so did the power and influence of the professional organizations. Lawyers who were products of an increasingly uniform approach to legal education could not help but emerge from the experience with a strong sense of camaraderie and shared interests, and with a loyalty to their profession that necessarily competed with other, more traditional, ethnic, religious, and class affinities.

Within church-related schools like USF, "the atmosphere of faith," which Henry Woods had called vital to Jesuit professional education, began to dissipate. The influence of the religious community on the curriculum diminished. Jesuits rarely appeared on the faculty rolls. Under pressure from the AALS, the regent system was abandoned and the power of the dean was thereby increased.

Ironically, it was one of the ABA's own inspectors who then turned on the Jesuit law schools, chastising them in 1954 because the religious aspect of a church-related legal education consisted of little more than an "external gloss." In a speech to the Association of Jesuit Law Schools, John Hervey asked, "Is it too much to expect that the full-time teachers in a church-related law school will be so imbued and so saturated with the philosophies, doctrines, and dogmas of the church that these will pour forth effortlessly in the classroom discussions in every course?"[8]

The answer was apparently yes. Hervey's implied concept of a lawyer/priest was realized only in the rarest individuals—Father Vachon, S.J., for example, who took his LL.B. in the late 1950s and then pursued a masters degree in law while teaching jurisprudence, or Father Paul P. Harbrecht, S.J. of Georgetown, who spoke at the Kendrick Hall dedication. Nevertheless, the atmosphere of faith continued to be an integral part of the USF experience. Faculty asserted that it manifested itself in the large proportion of graduates who turned to careers in the public sector, recognizing the time-honored, Jesuit-inspired value placed on service.

The dedication of Kendrick Hall occasioned considerable testimony to the continuing, even evolving, "atmosphere of faith" present at USF. When Hastings dedicated its new building at 198 McAllister Street in 1953, for example, the keynote speech was delivered by the president of the AALS, who focused on the evolution of legal education. Clark Kerr, the man who would become the chief architect of the University of

California's expansion and of the concept of the "multiversity," and who followed very closely in the footsteps of Henry Woods' nemesis, Benjamin Ide Wheeler, was there to congratulate Hastings on its accomplishments.

In contrast, the themes developed by the principal speakers at Kendrick Hall's dedication ceremonies went to the heart of what it meant to be a lawyer with a conscience. To be sure, the perspective was not unified. Father Harbrecht criticized the facelessness of ownership and government in America: "The people who make demands are not the ones who execute them... we are badly in need of a way of arriving at some means of public accountability, that is, some way for members of our society to review and to participate in the decisions that govern our lives."[9] Harbrecht declared that a new morality was in the making in America and pointed to the Civil Rights Commission, increased levels of foreign aid, and greater awareness of human relations as measures of the change.

Celebrating at the banquet held in the Grand Ballroom of the Fairmont Hotel following the dedication of Kendrick Hall, Charles Kendrick extends a hand to well-wishers. USF ARCHIVES/VANO PHOTOGRAPHY.

In contrast, San Francisco attorney Herman Phleger, a former legal adviser to the Department of State who keynoted the dedication on Saturday morning, dwelled on the significance of the Cold War. He asserted that in communist countries "there is no natural or moral law" and that in free countries the first line of domestic defense against the infiltration of communist ideas was the lawyer, whose principal responsibility was to protect the rights of individuals. Phleger's comments made for an interesting paraphrase of Alexis de Toqueville, who, in the mid-nineteenth century, described lawyers as the conservative social guardians of American democracy. Concluding his speech, Phleger called his peers and the attending law students to a higher purpose: "We must realize that our goal is not a life of personal comfort and amusement; we must make our country a living reality of justice under law."[10]

Indeed, there was no consensus of vision apparent in the

The center staircase in the law library in Kendrick Hall. Designed in the round, the Kendrick Hall library was supposed to afford the student easy access to all the materials in the library. USF ARCHIVES.

addresses given during the course of that September weekend—only a constant call to service. Racial tension on the campus of the University of Mississippi, precipitated by the court-ordered integration of the school, prevented Robert F. Kennedy from attending the dedication, but did not prevent him from speaking to the assembled crowd at the Fairmont by telephone. In his speech, Kennedy chastised the American Bar Association and the prominent attorneys of Mississippi: "I realize in that difficult social situation that to defend the fundamental principles of respect for the law and compliance with federal court orders would be unpopular and require great courage." "Nevertheless," he continued, "they still have their obligations as lawyers and they have remained silent." Kennedy ranked moral courage as the highest ideal of the profession and expressed his confidence that "the graduates who come out of Kendrick Hall in the long years of its future will be... lawyers courageously dedicated to the broadest horizons of citizenship and service. We will be waiting for them. We need them."[11]

Kennedy ranked moral courage as the highest ideal of the profession and expressed his confidence that "the graduates who come out of Kendrick Hall in the long years of its future will be... lawyers courageously dedicated to the broadest horizons of citizenship and service."

These explicit statements of faith were the testimony of what often went unsaid but was nevertheless felt by all who were a part of the University of San Francisco's School of Law as it entered a new era in the early 1960s. Among the alumni, the faculty, the students, and the university administrators, there was a feeling of tremendous pride and a sense that, after fifty years of struggle, a balance—between the university and the dean, the school and the professional organizations, the students and the faculty—had finally been achieved.

New facilities allowed for expansion, and, through the rest of the decade, enrollment in the law school increased steadily, from 223 in the fall of 1961 to 360 in the fall of 1967. The cumulative record on the bar between 1963 and 1968 was an impressive 77 percent. In 1962–1963, for the first time in thirty years, enrollment in the day school exceeded enrollment in the evening division. Each year thereafter, students in the day school accounted for a larger percentage of the overall total.

But in other ways, the law school did not change. USF undergraduates, for example, continued to account for more than a quarter of the law school's enrollment. The faculty grew, but remained relatively inbred; in 1964, six of sixteen had degrees from USF. The three-to-two ratio of Catholics to non-Catholics remained fairly constant, and no more than two dozen women each year were included on the student roster. Structural tensions between the university and the law school that were related to authority and purpose did not go away; they simply smoldered beneath the surface.

←600
ASHBURY
←1500
HAIGHT

CHAPTER IX

THE WIDEST STREET

THE SUPERFICIAL CALM that characterized American society in the 1950s and early 1960s disappeared in the middle of the decade. Increasing affluence fed expectations. Underlying tensions between races and generations erupted into confrontations between blacks and whites, students and university administrators, anti-war activists and political leaders. "We are beginning to go to confession as a nation," said USF alumnus Lewis H. Butler, then assistant secretary of the Department of Health, Education and Welfare.[1]

Like other institutions in America, the nation's law schools were rocked by the sixties. Student strikes and protests over issues as diverse as minority hiring, the war in Vietnam, student representation, and "relevant" education were ubiquitous. Increasingly politicized college students began applying to law school, hoping that a law degree would help them change the world. This factor, combined with the coming of age of the baby boomers, accounted for a dramatic increase in the number of people applying to law school. In the three years between 1968 and 1970 alone, applications to California law schools nearly doubled, while the number accepted increased by less than a quarter.

The counterculture revolution seemed to pivot around the corner of Haight and Ashbury streets. The Grateful Dead rocked to the pulse of what felt like a new generation. HERBIE GREENE, ROBERT KOCH GALLERY.

At USF, Frank Walsh completed his twelfth year as dean in the spring of 1969. His tenure in office thus equalled that of Edward Hogan and exceeded every other full-time academic dean before him. That fall, Walsh took a sabbatical leave, and, in his absence, Professor William J. Riegger became acting dean.

During the year that Riegger was dean, the anti-war movement reached its zenith. In October, more than a million people nationwide turned out to observe the Vietnam "moratorium." Then in May of 1970, with the announcement of the invasion of Cambodia, the campus revolt reached its climax: four students killed by National Guardsmen at Kent State; two black students shot down and eleven others wounded by highway patrolmen at Jackson State. The president of Columbia University called it "the most disastrous month of May in the history of American higher education."[2]

Students at USF grabbed fewer headlines than their peers at either U.C. Berkeley or San Francisco State, but their criticism was no less vocal. The provincial head of the Jesuit community, Father Patrick Donahue, S.J., visited the university on

Outside Kendrick Hall, students demonstrated in favor of minority and special-admissions programs. USF FORUM.

several occasions in 1968–1969 and heard complaints from students that the faculty, particularly the Jesuits, were aloof and insensitive to student calls for a more "relevant" curriculum. When Father President Charles W. Dullea, S.J., stepped down, Donahue sought to improve communication with the students by promoting a popular, relatively young Jesuit professor of philosophy, Father Albert Jonsen, S.J.

Father President Albert Jonsen. Promoted to the presidency in 1969, Jonsen attempted to implement university-wide reforms. He pushed for affirmative action, decreased the number of required courses in theology and philosophy, and oversaw the legal separation of the university from the Jesuit community. USF ARCHIVES/W. MURPHY, III.

THIRTY-EIGHT-YEAR-OLD Father Jonsen was an outspoken champion of the new era. As president, he supported the adoption of an affirmative action policy and the recruitment of minority students and faculty. He reduced the number of required courses in theology and philosophy. In keeping with a national policy among Jesuit institutions, and at the direction of Donahue, Jonsen initiated the legal separation of the university from the Jesuit community.[3]

Jonsen stimulated discussions about curriculum and challenged every department to evaluate its methods. In the law school, much of this discussion was aired in the newly created student-run newspaper, the *Forum*. In the first issue, published in April of 1970, faculty members Thomas McCarthy and Peter Donnici challenged the framework of the curriculum at USF and called for a more practical education aimed at integrating the curriculum into the community. "We are located in the middle of the most fantastic legal laboratory in the world," McCarthy wrote. "The City of San Francisco is a microcosm of all the joys, sicknesses and legal nightmares of 1970 America. But the city hardly touches our sacred Langdellian Ivory Tower."[4]

When the school year ended, Frank Walsh returned to USF only to announce that he had been offered and would accept a position at the Federal Communications Commission as head of the Broadcast Division. By this time, Riegger had already accepted a position on the faculty at Hastings. And so in the fall of 1970, A. Russell Berti, for the third time in his career, became acting dean of the USF School of Law.

For a man who was so much a part of the old guard, Berti showed remarkable flexibility in his last tenure as dean, especially given the times. The expansion of the student body from 361 in the fall of 1969 to 494 in the fall of 1970 created hundreds of administrative problems and fueled already existing tensions within the faculty and student body. Moreover, Berti was faced

Enrollments were projected to jump again in the fall of 1971 to almost 600 students, well above the number Kendrick Hall had been designed for. The faculty, which had not changed dramatically in size despite the addition of almost 250 students over the last two years, desperately needed to be increased.

with administering a student body that was dramatically different from any previous law school population. For the first time, Catholics did not make up the majority of the student body—in a single year, Catholic enrollment dropped from 55 percent to 45 percent. Women now accounted for 10 percent of the student body. The first-year class included fifteen minority students enrolled under a special-admissions program.

GIVEN ALL THESE CHANGES, it's not surprising that in the fall of 1970, a *Forum* poll revealed widespread student dissatisfaction with the lack of student representation on law school decision-making committees, the lack of scholarships based on need rather than merit, and the absence of student evaluations of faculty. Through it all, Berti responded with concern, respect, and humor. "I sense the vibes of certain persons readying to sound the charge for a student assault against the citadel,"[5] wrote the sixty-six-year-old dean in one issue of the *Forum*. Nevertheless, he supported many of the changes called for by students and faculty, adding electives to the curriculum and enhancing the clinical program.

Throughout the year that Berti was dean, for the first time in the law school's history, a dean search committee composed of alumni, faculty, and students looked for a successor to Walsh. Some members of the faculty and of the alumni objected to the fact that Father President Jonsen had authorized a nationwide search and did not place any restrictions on the candidate's religious beliefs, but the weight of history was not on their side.

In April, after almost a year's work, the selection committee came back to Jonsen with their candidate—the assistant dean of New York University (NYU), C. Delos Putz, Jr. Jonsen approved the recommendation, and Putz, a thirty-three-year-old graduate of NYU who specialized in corporate law, was hired in April of 1971.

Even before he left New York, Putz began preparing for the challenges at USF, and they were expected to be considerable. Enrollments were projected to jump again in the fall of 1971 to almost 600 students, well above the number Kendrick Hall had been designed for. The faculty, which had not changed dramatically in size despite the addition of almost 250 students over the last two years, desperately needed to be increased. To make matters worse, three of ten full-time teachers on the staff in 1970 were scheduled to leave or take sabbaticals in the fall of 1971. Thus, even before the school year began, Putz had to hire seven full-time faculty members, and these made up more than half of the faculty, including USF's first woman and first black law professor, Cheri Gaines.

With the explicit support of Father President Jonsen, Putz began a major expansion of the law school's services, curriculum, and faculty concomitant with the already expanded enrollment. In the *USF Alumnus* in autumn of 1971, after the new faculty appointments were announced, he stated, "This is just the beginning—the first step in planned expansion of the faculty to 20 or 21 full-time teachers within the next two years."[6]

Despite the changes he inaugurated, however, Putz reaffirmed the essential importance of the law school's roots and traditions. "Leading Catholic educational institutions have long since recognized that inculcation of religious doctrine is not an appropriate function of post-graduate professional education," he wrote in a letter to the *Forum*. "However, this is not to say that there is no appropriate role for 'Catholic' law schools." Echoing a number of the deans who had preceded him, Putz argued that the school's "special obligation" was to be socially conscious.[7]

Putz renewed the school's commitment to community service, which he felt should be a vital part of an urban law school's program. He pledged his support for minority special-admissions programs and sanctioned student representation on a number of faculty committees. To most of the students, as the *Forum* noted, Putz was a "man on the move," and, with the exception of a few who were concerned that all this change would undermine the school's performance on the bar, the students felt that USF would benefit by his leadership.

Throughout his first year as dean, student interest in the war, draft resistance, poverty law programs, and minority rights remained high. But in terms of the history of the law school itself, perhaps the most significant change of all began in the spring of 1972, when the law school undertook its own budget for the first time. Previously, no formal effort had been made to correlate law school expenses to law school income; the law school was simply treated as a department of the university. Under separate budgeting, the school was forced to match costs against income, and the university was forced to justify the overhead it charged the law school.

Over this last issue, problems arose immediately as students, faculty, the dean, and university officials attempted to

Law professor David A. Garcia in the early 1970s. A graduate of USF with an LL.M. from Yale, Garcia served as the managing attorney of the Mission Law Office of the San Francisco Neighborhood Legal Assistance Foundation. In 1983, Garcia was appointed as a Municipal Court Judge in San Francisco. USF ARCHIVES.

The reaction in the law school was one of outrage. Almost immediately, the Student Bar Association began preparing a lawsuit against the university.

determine a "fair share" of the university's expenses and debated whether these appropriately included such things as the athletic director's salary or the cost of student health services, for which law students were not eligible. In addition, the law school argued that it was entitled to credit its budget with some proportion of the funds donated to the university every year in the name of the law school. These issues became especially sensitive in light of the university's strained financial situation.

In 1972, a compromise budget was worked out; it included a university overhead charge of approximately $155,000. Unfortunately, the university's financial picture continued to deteriorate. Because of the changes Jonsen had made, particularly in carrying out the legal separation of the university from the Jesuit community, he lost support on the board of trustees, which was composed primarily of Jesuits. In the late spring of 1972, he resigned.

The man who succeeded Jonsen, after a six-month search by the board of trustees, became the first president of USF to be selected by committee rather than by the Father Provincial. Hired for his reputation as a budget balancer, William McInnes, S.J., began active duty at USF in January of 1973. One of his first tasks was to begin putting together the university budget for 1973–1974—and it would be a blockbuster.

In retrospect, the maelstrom of controversy that grew out of the 1973–1974 budget was again an example of how underlying institutional tensions swirling beneath the surface developed into conflicts under the influence of the times. In the end, the 1973–1974 budget pitted not only the law school against the university, but also the university against the ABA.

On March 1, 1973, Father McInnes announced a wage freeze, an 11 percent tuition hike, and drastic reductions in budgets for almost all departments. Included in the new budget for the law school was a $410,389 charge for university overhead, a 260 percent increase over the previous year. To finance this pass-along to the university, McInnes proposed to freeze faculty hiring, end financial aid for new special-admissions students, reduce aid for existing students, decrease the number of electives offered, and curtail library operations.

The reaction in the law school was one of outrage. Almost immediately the Student Bar Association began preparing a lawsuit against the university. When it became apparent that there would be no substantive concessions from the university administration, ten students filed suit, charging breach of contract, unjust enrichment, and fraud.

A major element of the controversy and the suit was the fact that the ABA-AALS accreditation team was scheduled to review the law school's standing in 1973. The students used the accreditation process to argue in their briefs that the university's actions endangered the value of their degree. Dean Putz, on the other hand, looked to the accreditation team for support in his fight with McInnes. In a report sent to the ABA-AALS in March, he outlined his objections to the university's budget and stated, "It does not appear that this 'share of general university overhead' was calculated on any basis other than the financial need of the university."[8]

When the university increased the law school's share of university overhead to more than $400,000, students filed suit, charging breach of contract. The suit's settlement had far-reaching consequences for the law school's future. USF ARCHIVES.

Also at issue was the question of whether the law school would be allowed to conduct its own development campaign. Putz and other members of the law school community realized that the ability of the law school to raise funds independent of the university was critical to the physical expansion of Kendrick Hall and central to any question of the law school's autonomy. In the spring of 1972, Father Jonsen had agreed to allow the dean of the law school to solicit funds earmarked for law school programs. But when McInnes took office, he rescinded that agreement.

Against the background of the ongoing Watergate investigation, the students and the dean pursued their separate battles against Father President McInnes through the summer and into the fall of 1973. The faculty, endeavoring to pursue their interests within the budget controversy independent of the dean and the students, organized a union. Then in September, Presiding Judge Joseph Karesh ordered the students and the university to participate in a settlement conference.

An out-of-court settlement was signed on October 31. Among other things, it reinstated the university's promise to increase the full-time faculty to twenty-two in the fall of 1974, reinstated $25,000 for financial aid for the spring semester, and committed the university to hiring a full-time placement officer. The settlement provided funds for the maintenance of the number of elective courses offered in the fall of 1972 and, most importantly, allowed the law school to conduct an independent fundraising campaign, the proceeds of which would be used only for the law school. While the students' attorney, James Lorenz, stipulated that "it would be a mistake to look at the settlement as a victory," the settlement, nevertheless, contributed a great deal to increasing the school's autonomy; the rest would have to wait for the professional associations.[9]

In the fall of 1973, the accreditation team returned its report. As expected, it was critical; in particular, it questioned the sincerity of the university's commitment to quality legal education at USF. The report asked for further information, but as President McInnes wrote in an article published in the *Forum*, "Corrections and statements took second place, in the eyes of the review committee, to concrete commitments, especially financial."[10]

In some ways, USF's troubles were not unique. Given the demand for legal education in the early seventies, law school profits were a temptation to other universities as well. The Council of the Section on Legal Education of the ABA was concerned about the problem generally, and this concern partly explains the tough stand they took with USF.

In December, Dean Putz and Provost Seidl appeared before the council to respond to the accreditation team's report. When it became apparent that neither one had the authority to make the promises the council was looking for, the members asked to see McInnes himself. In February, the dean and the president were called to Houston. At that point, McInnes and Putz were hardly speaking to each other.

In a closed-door meeting, the council tried to pin McInnes down, asking him particularly whether the university would enable the law school to raise salaries to an adequate level and to hire enough full-time faculty to reduce the student/teacher ratio. McInnes argued that he did not have the authority to make those promises and that he would need to consult his board of trustees. Reportedly, the chairman of the council told the president, "Very well, Father McInnes, there's a phone booth out in the hall. We'll give you thirty minutes to get the authority."[11]

In the end, the president and the board caved in, but apparently not without some serious consideration of surrendering the law school's accreditation. Promises were made to hire four new faculty members in the fall of 1974. Enrollment was to be limited to preserve a 34:1 student/faculty ratio. Salaries were to be increased to meet the national law school median by 1976. The council, for its part, agreed to continue the law school's accreditation on a probationary basis with the understanding that the school's progress would be monitored.

Seemingly, the controversy was ended. But in November, the *Forum* reported that the university would not renew the dean's contract. And in the spring, the university asserted its authority further by attempting to deny promotions to three law school professors whose promotions had been recommended by the Law School Faculty Status Committee. Some people in the law school felt that McInnes was taking his revenge. Indeed, it would be years before the suspicions and accusations died down and the relationship between the university and the law school returned to some kind of equilibrium.

Under a compromise agreement, Putz did resign the deanship and took a year's leave of absence in the spring of 1975. Under his administration, inherent conflicts over authority that had existed between the university and the law school—and the university and the professional associations—for more than forty years had finally come to a head. As a result, the law school had increased its autonomy significantly, to the point where some believed that the law school and its policies were completely divorced from the problems and concerns of the university and the church. Events would prove that this was not the case.

Retirements and sabbaticals combined to transform the law school faculty in 1971. Dean C. Delos Putz hired seven new full-time faculty members to fill the accumulated vacancies. The entire faculty is pictured here. Back, from left to right: Francis Walsh, Eldon Reiley, Jack Bonanno, Joseph Henke, James Cox, J. Thomas McCarthy, Cherie Gaines, Ted Rhodes, Elizabeth Anne Quigley. Front, from left to right: Dean C. Delos Putz, Stan Darling, and Raymond Coyne. USF ARCHIVES.

CHAPTER X

LOOKING FORWARD

THE END OF THE SIXTIES came not with the formal end of the decade but in the summer and fall of 1974, when Richard Nixon resigned the presidency and the OPEC oil embargo placed a stranglehold on the American economy. The literal and figurative "big chill" that began that winter was noted by the press as the country, badly shaken by almost a decade of civil violence and turmoil, took stock of itself and attempted to return to some kind of equilibrium.

Even without the protests, however, the social revolution went forward, marked by the rapidly evolving character of sex roles, the family, and the workplace. Fundamental relationships—between whites and minorities, men and women, teachers and students—had all been changed at least superficially, if not substantively.

By 1974, the baby boomers, for the most part, had passed through the nation's universities, and enrollment in undergraduate programs began to decline. At the same time, law school enrollments continued to increase—exceeding 126,000 in 1977. The student population of most law schools, including USF, was increasingly composed of a curious combination of younger, more conservative students mixed with slightly older, more politicized students—like Gary Trudeau's comic-strip character Joanie Caucus—who, after having experimented with some alternative lifestyles and/or politics, came back to school believing that a law degree was the key to making a difference in America.

Despite the controversies, the increasing number of minority students at USF was some indication of the success of the school's recruitment policies. Pictured here, graduate Patricia Poole and her family. USF ARCHIVES.

These students, some of whom had learned the techniques of direct action in college, asserted themselves in a way unparalleled in the history of legal education in the United States. With the war over, they turned their attention to issues closer to home, fighting for minority admissions and making clear their dissatisfaction with the curriculum and the Langdellian case method of instruction. They came looking for an education that would offer greater insight into the relationships between law and society. And, like legal realists of the 1930s, they demanded an education which was as much philosophical as it was practical.

For law school administrators, it was an extremely difficult era. While they were trying to reform the curriculum to take into account the needs of public-interest-oriented students and faculty, they were attacked by the bar, the judiciary, and their own alumni for failing to provide the basics of legal education. Bar pass rates, which had remained high through most of the sixties, took a sudden nose dive in the middle

Senator Sam Ervin during a visit to campus. USF ARCHIVES.

seventies. Some prominent members of the bar, led by Chief Justice Warren Burger, charged that law schools were neglecting the basic skills of lawyering. They looked with suspicion at the proliferating number of electives and argued instead for required courses in legal writing and trial advocacy.[1]

Indeed, in the aftermath of the sixties, law schools struggled as never before with the inherent dialectic of legal education: whether to teach the skills necessary for practice and passing the bar exam, or whether to emphasize legal theory and teach understanding of the law as an intellectual endeavor.

Indeed, in the aftermath of the sixties, law schools struggled as never before with the inherent dialectic of legal education: whether to teach the skills necessary for practice and passing the bar exam, or whether to emphasize legal theory and teach understanding of the law as an intellectual endeavor.

ONCE AGAIN, there was a call for increased standards. But increasing standards was not quite the straightforward task it had been in the thirties, forties, and fifties. For one thing, law schools seemed more and more resistant to flunking students out. In the mid-sixties, the attrition rate had been close to 45 percent; by the late seventies, it had dropped to 13 percent. Moreover, law schools argued they shouldn't have to flunk people; more competitive admissions meant superior students who should all be able to make the grade. But the fact remained that at USF, for example, the bottom fifth of the class at times had a pass rate below 10 percent.

Making the whole issue of raising standards even more complicated was the issue of special admissions. In the late sixties and early seventies, most law schools had recognized the inequities implicit in the severe shortage of minority group lawyers and had adopted special-admissions programs. At USF, the program was so progressive that it ranked second in the nation among private law schools. But by the middle of the decade, when these special-admissions students began to take the bar, it became clear that the school had not been able to provide enough extra support to enable these students to make the grade.

At USF, the issue became particularly divisive after the school's average on the summer 1976 bar exam plunged to 62.5 percent, compared to a five-year average of 78.7 percent. A committee appointed by Dean Paul McKaskle determined that special-admissions students had performed especially poorly. As a result, many alumni and some students, fearing the school's reputation would suffer, put pressure on the dean to make changes.

McKaskle had been appointed dean following Putz's resignation in February of 1975. A 1963 graduate of U.C. Berkeley, McKaskle was certainly not unsympathetic to the need for a special-admissions program. Before coming to USF in 1971, he had served as the director of litigation at the Western Center on Law and Poverty in Los Angeles, and on many occasions he expressed his support for the program's intent.

Nevertheless, the dean felt that the school was clearly not capable of supporting the program it was attempting. He argued that special-admissions students were thus suffering a further injustice, and that a low bar pass rate hurt the reputation of the entire school, cheapening the degrees of all other students and graduates. He proposed a substantial cutback in the program.[2]

Student reaction to the dean's proposal was loud and vociferous. The Supreme Court decision in the *Bakke* case, which had been decided that same year, made the program's future seem all the more precarious. On two different occasions, students demonstrated outside Kendrick Hall in support of special admissions. Again, in this battle, USF was not alone; similar demonstrations took place at Hastings and Boalt that year.

Despite the chanting on the front steps, McKaskle tried to take a long view of the law school's future. In taking over the deanship in 1975 in the wake of the student lawsuit and the

When Dean Paul McKaskle proposed substantial cutbacks in special admissions and funding for special-admissions support programs, students took to Fulton Street to protest. FORUM.

bitter accreditation process, McKaskle had inherited powerful tools for reconstructing the framework of the law school. Most important of these was the school's new ability to organize its own fundraising.

In 1975, shortly after he was appointed permanent dean, McKaskle began working with Tom Jordan, the man who had organized the university's "Second Century" campaign, to establish a stable funding base for the school that would protect its independence and support its continued growth. Essential to that effort was the participation of the school's alumni.

IN THE SPRING OF 1976, an initial Board of Advisors was invited into the law school to undertake a one-time study, to talk to faculty, staff, and students, and to attempt to come up with an objective perspective on the strengths and weaknesses of the school. The board included some alumni, but also included managers from industry and government.

One outgrowth of the Board of Advisors was the creation of an independent Board of Counselors created to provide ongoing advice to the dean and to help build external support, both financial and moral, for the school. Both Jordan and McKaskle saw the Board of Counselors as critical to the

In 1971, members of the Environmental Law Society (ELS) opposed the construction of Sutro Tower and filed a lawsuit contending that the tower had not been properly approved by city officials. Here, Dean Paul McKaskle and members of the ELS discuss the court's decision. FORUM/JOSEPH J ROSENTHAL.

GEORGE A. HELMER

When Dean Paul McKaskle and Development Officer Tom Jordan began to organize the law school's Board of Counselors, they felt they needed one man who could give the new organization credibility and weight. The man they found was George Helmer. According to McKaskle, "George was a grand old man of law in San Francisco and a lot of people were impressed when he made his pitch for the law school."

Born in Berkeley, Helmer graduated from the University of San Francisco in 1936 and earned his degree from the School of Law in 1940. He served as an officer in naval air intelligence during World War II, returned to San Francisco to work for a year as deputy city attorney, and thereafter joined the firm of Cooper, White and Cooper. For a number of years, Helmer taught as an adjunct professor at USF. He was an accomplished and demanding teacher.

In 1961, Helmer went to the East Coast and for eleven years served as senior vice president, general counsel, and a director of Engelhard Minerals and Chemicals Corporation. In 1973, he returned to San Francisco, becoming a partner at Cullinan, Brown and Helmer.

When the Board of Counselors of the School of Law was founded in 1977, George Helmer served as the founding chairman. Helmer encouraged a free-wheeling discussion of law school affairs and was instrumental in securing the participation of a number of respected lawyers and judges. When Paul McKaskle stepped down as dean of the law school, George Helmer played an important part in the selection of the new dean, David Ratner.

He led the law school's successful fund drive, which raised over a million dollars to underwrite the addition of a new wing to Kendrick Hall. Helmer also endowed a scholarship fund at the law school. In 1980, he received the university's St. Thomas More Award.

When Helmer died in 1983, Dean David Ratner said of him, "No institution has ever had a better friend. He not only gave generously of his time and wisdom to the school, he was totally dedicated to its advancement."

school's future and looked long and hard for a single individual who would catalyze the board's creation. The man they found was George Helmer.

Helmer was a graduate of both the university and the law school at USF. He had been a member of the faculty from 1946 to 1951 and, for eleven years, served as senior vice president, general counsel, and a director of Engelhard Minerals and Chemicals of New Jersey. He had an outstanding reputation in the legal community. When he agreed to take the lead in organizing an ongoing Board of Counselors for the law school, Helmer virtually assured its success.

In 1977, Kendrick Hall was drastically overcrowded. Enrollment was up to 760 students. Full-time faculty did not have adequate offices. Space for the growing administrative staff, particularly the placement and alumni relations office, was at a premium. Consequently, one of the first priorities established by the Board of Counselors was to raise money to enable the school to expand.

When law school enrollments exploded in the 1970s, overcrowding at Kendrick Hall became severe. A successful fund-raising drive led by the Board of Counselors underwrote the construction and completion of the school's new wing in 1982. USF ARCHIVES.

It was Henke's intention, shared by the faculty, to go ahead with the implementation of plans and programs aimed at making USF a "good place and a better place to study law."

IN 1978, the university flirted with the idea of relocating part or all of the law school to the newly acquired buildings on Lone Mountain, but decided against the move. Instead, plans for an addition to Kendrick Hall were drawn up, and a fundraising campaign designed to raise almost a million dollars was launched.

Shortly after the plans for a new addition were announced in the spring of 1979, Paul McKaskle informed the law school community that he would step down as dean as soon as the university could complete a search for a replacement. According to McKaskle, he was tired of administrative work and wanted to return to full-time teaching.

THE PROCESS OF SELECTING an acceptable candidate, however, turned out to be quite difficult. In February of 1980, Robert Yegge, former dean of the University of Denver College of Law, was offered and accepted the position. Plans were made for a transition of administrations, and Paul McKaskle announced his intention to take a sabbatical upon Yegge's assumption of office. But on March 20, Yegge was arrested in Denver on vice charges, and shortly thereafter resigned his appointment to the deanship.

In the aftermath of the Yegge affair, the search for a new dean continued. McKaskle stayed on at the helm through the spring and fall of 1980, overseeing the fundraising campaign for the new wing and increasing the school's endowment funding during a period when the rest of the university was in severe financial trouble.

In December, when McKaskle was scheduled to leave on sabbatical, Joseph Henke, a member of the faculty since 1970, stepped in to serve as acting dean. A graduate of Amherst and the University of Washington's School of Law, Henke was a soft-spoken administrator who was popular with students and faculty alike. Nevertheless, he tried to make it clear that his administration would not take a caretaker position. It was his intention, shared by the faculty, to go ahead with the implementation of plans and programs aimed at making USF a "good place and a better place to study law."[3]

In many ways, the situation Henke faced was promising: the bar pass rate over the past two years had averaged over 70 percent; within weeks of his appoinment, jackhammers signalled the beginning of construction on the new wing. Despite Henke's enthusiasm, however, the sense of stalemate persisted, particularly as rumors circulated that the dean search committee had found a candidate, only to lose him because the university administration was not willing to make promises about the budget. An article in the April 30, 1981, edition of the *Forum* quoted one faculty member as saying "student morale has never been lower."

The 1981–1982 academic year was well under way when Professor Steven Shatz walked into the office of visiting professor David Ratner and asked him if he still had an interest in being dean. Ratner had interviewed for the job in the fall of 1979. In the fall of 1980, he had come to USF as a Marshall P. Madison Visiting Professor, and returned to USF for another semester in the fall of 1981. Ratner told Shatz he would consider the position.

Hired in the fall of 1981, David Ratner taught law at Cornell for eighteen years before accepting the deanship at USF. With enrollments and applications down nationwide, Ratner has emphasized a practical and prudent approach to both curriculum and financial planning. USF ARCHIVES/RICHARD CHATCUFF.

Ratner appealed to students, faculty, and the administration alike because his credentials were impeccable: a graduate of Harvard College and Law School, he was a prominent authority on securities law and had taught at Cornell for eighteen years. He described himself as a pragmatist and a realist, rather than an ideologue, and professed a relaxed administrative style. His acceptance of the job in the fall of 1981 brought a welcome sigh of relief to the entire school and ended what had effectively been a three-year search for a dean.

In the nearly five years that David Ratner has been dean, significant changes have taken place in legal education. The great demand that characterized the 1970s has dissipated. Government-sponsored financial aid has been reduced. Smaller private schools like USF, still scrambling to put in place significant endowment funds, have been caught between their need to maintain tuition revenue and their desire to uphold standards for admission and retention. This effort has been particularly difficult given the diminishing pool of applicants.[4]

Ratner has worked with the faculty, the alumni, the students, and the university to reshape the school in a way that he hopes will maintain its viability in the years to come. Two principal components of that strategy have been to reduce the size of the student body to preserve its quality and to increase the school's endowment from $250,000 in 1982 to almost $5,000,000 by 1987, thus making the school less vulnerable to fluctuations in tuition income.[5]

In 1982–1983, the faculty held a retreat to revise the curriculum to place a greater emphasis on teaching skills. Out of that retreat came major curriculum revisions, including the

Three generations of law school graduates: George H. Sullivan ('23); Kenneth R. Sullivan ('60); and George R. Sullivan ('89). USF LAWYER/RICHARD CHATCUFF.

introduction of a year-long Lawyering Process course. In some ways, the changes have apparently paid off, as more and more USF graduates have been accepted into competitive positions with major law firms. But the school's bar pass rate has slipped again to a three-year average of just over 50 percent.

Like Deans Kinnane, Miller, and Walsh before him, Ratner's answer has been to attempt to accept only clearly capable applicants and to eliminate weak students. Indeed, in the fall of 1986, Ratner proposed a 20 percent attrition rate, basing his proposal on the dramatically poor performance of the bottom "quintile" of each class on the bar. Further, the dean proposed eliminating special admissions in favor of recruiting qualified minority applicants.

Student reaction to the dean's proposal has been less dramatic than in previous years, but no less concerned. Year to year, an ambivalence with regard to the elite versus the democratic elements of the USF tradition permeates the law school student body and manifests itself in stubborn resistance to a return to the narrowly focused but extremely purposeful mood that characterized the law school in the late fifties and early sixties.

SINCE THAT HOT September evening in 1912 when the first class of St. Ignatius law students met in the Grant Building on Market Street, tremendous changes have overtaken the legal profession. Nevertheless, the issues that have plagued legal education and particularly the University of San Francisco's School of Law throughout the last seventy-five years are almost all still alive and extremely vigorous.

As Dean Ratner and the law school faculty attempt to redefine the law school's mission in practical terms reminiscent of those articulated by the school's founders, the school finds it increasingly difficult to keep up with the ever-escalating standards of the ABA and the AALS. Indeed, Ratner compares this era to the first decades of this century when the professional associations made a concerted effort to drive the night schools out of business. Ironically, as Ratner points out, the effort may backfire. "In recent years the bar pass rates for unaccredited schools in California, schools which do not have to spend money according to the dictates of the ABA and the AALS, have been improving, while scores for the non-elite, ABA-approved schools have been dropping."[6] Whatever USF's fu-

In 1968, women accounted for less than 10% of the students at the USF School of Law. By 1986, for the first time in the school's history, women in the first year class outnumbered men. USF ARCHIVES/RICHARD CHATCUFF.

ture, it seems certain that the accrediting institutions will continue to exert a strong influence.

Ratner's perspective on the school's future is not shared unanimously by the law school's community of students, faculty, and alumni. There are those who believe that the measure of a law school's program is the record of its graduates on the bar exam, and these people have become increasingly concerned at the school's recent pass rate. And for others, there still remains some question of whether the school has a unique role to play in legal education because of its religious affiliation.

Ambivalence lingers in the minds of many of the members of the faculty, the alumni, and the administration as well. For as the school enters the year of its seventy-fifth anniversary, its rich history creates a kind of conscience that seems to be an intangible element of all decision making: how to preserve the sense of intimacy, of mutual concern and respect, that has been so much a part of the school's history; how to provide opportunity to students who, for a hundred different reasons, might not otherwise be able to afford or take time out to go to law school; and how to maintain the kind of standards that have given rise to such a strong sense of pride and collective accomplishment among the entire law school community.

There are no easy solutions, and perhaps there are no solutions at all. For however one interprets "faith," the effort to teach law in an atmosphere of faith will forever remain a greater challenge than to teach it simply as a trade. Indeed, no matter how wide the street that separates the rest of the University of San Francisco from Kendrick Hall, this tradition of faith will always be a part of the law school's heritage and an important aspect of its contribution to the city of San Francisco.

GRADUATES OF USF SCHOOL OF LAW WHO HAVE HELD JUDICIAL OFFICE

(All positions are in California unless otherwise noted. The position listed is the highest judicial office held by each person; many also served on lower courts for substantial periods of time.)

1916
HON. C. HAROLD CAULFIELD★
Judge, Superior Court
City and County of San Francisco
1956–1971

1916
HON. JOSEPH M. GOLDEN★
Judge, Municipal Court
City and County of San Francisco
1923–1959

1918
HON. WILLIAM F. TRAVERSO★
Judge, Superior Court
City and County of San Francisco
1945–1965

1920
HON. EDWARD MOLKENBUHR★
Judge, Superior Court
City and County of San Francisco
1949–1960

1921
HON. MELVYN I. CRONIN★
Judge, Superior Court
City and County of San Francisco
1944–1977

1921
HON. JORDAN L. MARTINELLI★
Judge, Superior Court
Marin County
1949–1961

1922
HON. HERMAN A. VAN DER ZEE★
Judge, Superior Court
City and County of San Francisco
1947–1972

1923
HON. WILLIAM EDMUND SCOTT★
Judge, Superior Court
San Mateo County
1946–1971

1923
HON. WILLIAM T. SWEIGERT★
Judge, United States District Court
Northern District of California
1959–1983

1925
HON. JOHN J. MCMAHON
Judge, Municipal Court
City and County of San Francisco

1926
HON. GEORGE B. HARRIS★
Chief Judge, United States District Court
Northern District of California
1961–1970

1926
HON. WILLIAM A. O'BRIEN★
Judge, Superior Court
City and County of San Francisco
1963–1970

1927
HON. PRESTON DEVINE
Presiding Judge, Court of Appeal
First Appellate District, Division Four
1966–1974

1927
HON. NORMAN H. ELKINGTON
Associate Justice, Court of Appeal
First Appellate District, Division One
1966–

1928
HON. HAROLD J. HALEY★
Judge, Superior Court
Marin County
1965–1971

1928
HON. FRANK J. MACKIN
Judge, Superior Court
Los Angeles County
1961–1971

1929
HON. LELAND J. LAZARUS
Judge, Superior Court
City and County of San Francisco
1965–1974

1929
HON. CHARLES J. MCGOLDRICK
Judge, Superior Court
Sonoma County
1951–1968

1930
HON. BYRON ARNOLD
Judge, Superior Court
City and County of San Francisco
1955–1971

1930
HON. FRANK J. COMAICH★
Judge, Municipal Court
San Mateo County
1960–1973

1930
HON. RAYMOND L. SULLIVAN
Associate Justice, Supreme Court of California
1966–1973

1931
HON. JOHN J. FAHEY★
Judge, Municipal Court
San Mateo County
1940–1949

1931
HON. GEORGE E. MALONEY★
Judge, Municipal Court
City and County of San Francisco
1961–1976

1931
HON. RAYMOND J. O'CONNOR★
Judge, Superior Court
City and County of San Francisco
1964–1969

1932
HON. RALPH V. DE VOTO★
Judge, Superior Court
Lake County
1969–1983

1932
HON. HUGH F. MULLIN, JR.
Judge, Justice Court
San Mateo County
1934–1949

1933
HON. LOUIS B. DEMATTEIS
Judge, Superior Court
San Mateo County
1953–1973

1933
HON. JOSEPH KARESH
Judge, Superior Court
City and County of San Francisco
1960–1978

1933
HON. JOHN B. MOLINARI
Presiding Justice, Court of Appeal
First Appellate District, Division One
1962–1976

1935
HON. ARTHUR J. ANDERSON
Judge, Superior Court
Lassen County
1973–1979

1936
HON. EDWARD O'DAY, JR.★
Judge, Superior Court
City and County of San Francisco
1960–1972

1938
HON. RUSSELL ZACHES
Judge, Municipal Court
Monterey County

1940
HON. THOMAS F. MCBRIDE
Judge, Superior Court
Contra Costa County
1965–1981

★deceased

Photo: USF ARCHIVES/JOHN GORMAN.

1941
Hon. Agnes O'Brien Smith★
Presiding Judge, Municipal Court
City and County of San Francisco
1970–1978

1944
Hon. Thomas E. Feeney
Judge, Superior Court
City and County of San Francisco
1966–1967

1944
Hon. W. Lee Vavuris
Judge, Superior Court
City and County of San Francisco
1971–1982

1945
Hon. Mark N. Olds
Judge, District Court
Third Circuit, State of Hawaii

1946
Hon. Robert J. Duggan
Judge, Municipal Court
Bay Judicial District
1959–1979

1946
Hon. Roger D. Foley
Chief Judge, United States District Court
District of Nevada
1963–1980

1946
Hon. Kenneth L. Lewis
Judge, District One
Kitsap County, State of Washington

1946
Hon. James C. Walsh, Jr.
Judge, Municipal Court
Alameda County
1977–

1947
Hon. Nat O. Bradley
Judge, Superior Court
Tulare County
1971–

1947
Hon. Dan B. Eymann
Judge, Municipal Court
Fresno County
1954–1977

1947
Hon. Lewis P. May
Judge, Municipal Court
Alameda County
1969–

1947
Hon. Frederick J. Woelflen
Chief Magistrate, United States District Court
Northern District of California
1978–

1948
Hon. Walter F. Calcagno★
Judge, Superior Court
City and County of San Francisco
1969–1985

1948
Hon. Robert E. Carey
Judge, Superior Court
San Mateo County
1971–

1948
Hon. Robert J. Drewes★
Judge, Superior Court
City and County of San Francisco
1966–1980

1948
Hon. Lyle R. Edson
Judge, Superior Court
San Mateo County
1969–1983

1948
Hon. Timothy W. O'Brien
Judge, Superior Court
Mendocino County
1971–1985

1948
Hon. Roy G. Pucci
Judge, Municipal Court
Alameda County
1966–

1948
Hon. Daniel A. Quinlan
Judge, District Court
Nez Perce County, Idaho
1970–1973

1948
Hon. Allison M. Rouse
Associate Justice, Court of Appeal
First Appellate District, Division Two
1971–

1949
Hon. George E. McDonald
Judge, Municipal Court
Alameda County
1966–1985

1949
Hon. Frank Piombo
Judge, Superior Court
San Mateo County
1971–

1950
Hon. Frank J. Creede, Jr.
Judge, Superior Court
Fresno County
1973–

1950
Hon. Carl P. Evans
Judge, Municipal Court
Fresno County
1979–

1950
Hon. Kiernan R. Hyland
Judge, Municipal Court
Sonoma County
1972–1981

1950
Hon. James E. Jones, Jr.★
Judge, Municipal Court
Sonoma County
1972–1981

1950
Hon. E. Warren McGuire
Judge, Superior Court
Marin County
1968–

1951
Hon. Joseph G. Babich
Judge, Superior Court
Sacramento County
1964–1984

1951
Hon. Clifford B. Bachand
Judge, Municipal Court
Alameda County
1976–

1951
Hon. James G. Changaris
Judge, Superior Court
Sutter County
1972–1978

1951
Hon. R. Donald Chapman
Judge, Superior Court
Santa Clara County
1980–

1951
Hon. Arthur Eissenger
Judge, Municipal Court
Sacramento County
1966–

1951
Hon. Robert Fairwell
Judge, Municipal Court
Alameda County
1965–

1951
Hon. Donald R. Fretz
Judge, Superior Court
Merced County
1963–

1951
Hon. Michael L. McInnis
Judge, Superior Court
Solano County
1979–

1951
Hon. Alexander J. McMahon★
Judge, Municipal Court
Sonoma County
1966–1976

1951
Hon. Frank S. Petersen
Judge, Superior Court
Del Norte County
1966–

1951
Hon. Wroy F. Renaghan★
Judge, Municipal Court
Mount Diablo County
1963–1973

1951
Hon. Donald W. Smith
Judge, Superior Court
San Diego County
1979–

1951
Hon. Peter A. Smith
Judge, Superior Court
Marin County
1978–

1951
Hon. Carson N. Taylor
Judge, Municipal Court
Stanislaus County
1977–1984

1952
Hon. Frank E. Hart
Judge, Superior Court
City and County of San Francisco
1984–

1952
Hon. Robert F. Kane
Justice, Court of Appeal
First Appellate District, Division Two
1971–1979

1952
Hon. Winton McKibben
Judge, Superior Court
Alameda County
1976–

1952
Hon. Owen E. Woodruff, Jr.
Chief Magistrate,
United States District Court
Northern District of California
1981–1984

1952
Hon. Douglas R. Woodworth
Judge, Superior Court
San Diego County
1972–

1953
Hon. John J. Boskovich
Judge, Superior Court
Tulare County
1971–

1953
Hon. Peter M. Elliott
Judge, United States Bankruptcy Court
Orange County
1970–

1953
Hon. Lawrence W. Marvin
Judge, Superior Court
Sacramento County
1985–

1953
Hon. Leonard H. McBride
Judge, Superior Court
Orange County
1979–

1953
Hon. Claude D. Perasso
Judge, Superior Court
City and County of San Francisco
1974–

1953
Hon. Frank W. Shaw
Judge, Superior Court
City and County of San Francisco
1971–

1954
Hon. Thomas F. Curtin
Judge, Municipal Court
Bay Judicial District
1973–

1954
Hon. John A. Ertola
Judge, Superior Court
City and County of San Francisco
1970–

1954
Hon. Richard D. Gravelle★
Judge, Municipal Court
San Mateo County
1984–1986

1954
Hon. Leighton Hatch
Judge, Municipal Court
Sacramento County
1974–

1954
Hon. Dorothy Von Beroldingen
Judge, Municipal Court
City and County of San Francisco
1977–

1955
Hon. John E. Benson
Associate Justice, Court of Appeal
First Appellate District, Division Two
1986–

1955
Hon. Raymond H. Simmons
Judge, Municipal Court
Monterey County
1974–

1957
Hon. Richard C. Garner
Judge, Superior Court
San Bernardino County
1971–

1958
Hon. Herbert L. Ashby
Associate Justice, Court of Appeal
Second Appellate District, Division Five
1972–

1958
Hon. Marie Bertillon Collins
Judge, Superior Court
Alameda County
1982–

1958
Hon. Donald B. King
Associate Justice, Court of Appeal
First Appellate District, Division Five
1982–

1958
Hon. G. Dave Teja
Judge, Municipal Court
Sutter County
1976–1978

1959
Hon. John J. Bible
Judge, Superior Court
San Mateo County
1978–

1959
Hon. Coleman Fannin
Judge, Superior Court
Contra Costa County
1972–

1959
Hon. William F. Lanam
Judge, Superior Court
San Mateo County
1973–

1959
Hon. Dominique Olcomendy
Judge, Municipal Court
City and County of San Francisco
1974–

1960
Hon. Charles E. Aguilar
Judge, Municipal Court
Stanislaus County
1977–

1960
Hon. Thomas J. Dandurand
Judge, Superior Court
City and County of San Francisco
1971–

1960
Hon. Joseph A. Desmond
Judge, Municipal Court
City and County of San Francisco
1983–

1960
Hon. Robert L. Dossee
Judge, Superior Court
City and County of San Francisco
1979–

1960
Hon. Patrick D. Gilroy
Judge, Circuit Court
Fifth Judicial District, State of Oregon
1974–

1960
Hon. Harold E. Neville, Jr.
Judge, Municipal Court
Humboldt County
1972–

1961
Hon. George T. Choppelas
Judge, Municipal Court
City and County of San Francisco
1982–

1961
Hon. Richard Figone
Judge, Superior Court
City and County of San Francisco
1981–

1961
Hon. William J. Mallen
Judge, Municipal Court
City and County of San Francisco
1982–

1961
Hon. Gary W. Thomas
Judge, Superior Court
Marin County
1986–

★deceased

1962
Hon. William F. Ferroggiaro, Jr.
Judge, Superior Court
Humboldt County
1983–

1962
Hon. Frank C. Francis
Judge, Superior Court
Nevada County
1971–

1962
Hon. Barry Hammer
Judge, Superior Court
San Luis Obispo County
1985–

1962
Hon. Frank J. Passalacqua
Judge, Municipal Court
Sonoma County
1964–

1963
Hon. Terence J. Keeley
Judge, Superior Court
Sutter County
1978–

1963
Hon. Raymond D. Williamson
Judge, Superior Court
City and County of San Francisco
1985–

1963
Hon. Ernest C. Zunino
Judge, Municipal Court
Marin County
1982–

1964
Hon. J. Michael Brown
Judge, Superior Court
Humboldt County
1982–

1964
Hon. Daniel M. Hanlon
Judge, Superior Court
City and County of San Francisco
1978–

1964
Hon. Charles R. Tunley
Judge, Superior Court
Nome, Alaska

1965
Hon. John J. Gallagher
Judge, Superior Court
Sonoma County
1976–

1965
Hon. Robert J. O'Neill
Judge, Superior Court
San Diego County
1980–

1965
Hon. Robert L. Schouweiler
Judge, District Court
Second Judicial District, State of Nevada
1981–

1966
Hon. Terrance R. Duncan
Commissioner, Municipal Court
Monterey County
1982–

1966
Hon. James S. White
Judge, Municipal Court
Alameda County
1979–

1967
Hon. Le Roy A. Simmons
Judge, Superior Court
San Bernardino County
1981–

1968
Hon. Michael R. Griffin
Judge, District Court
Carson County, Nevada
1979–

1968
Hon. Runston Maino
Judge, Municipal Court
San Diego County
1982–

1969
Hon. John M. Allen
Judge, Municipal Court
Contra Costa County
1984–

1969
Hon. James D. Garbolino
Judge, Superior Court
Placer County
1984–

1969
Hon. Steven D. McMorris
Judge, Tahoe Township Justice Court
Douglas County, Nevada
1982–

1970
Hon. David A. Garcia
Judge, Municipal Court
City and County of San Francisco
1983–

1970
Hon. Raymond J. Giordano
Judge, Superior Court
Sonoma County
1985–

1970
Hon. Eric R. Uldall
Judge, Municipal Court
Solano County
1984–

1971
Hon. Clifford L. Nakea
Judge, District Court
Fifth Circuit, State of Hawaii
1978–

1972
Hon. Lorenzo Arredondo
Judge, Municipal Court
Lake County
1976–

1972
Hon. Stephen Drew
Judge, Justice Court
Tulare County
1978–

1972
Hon. William R. McGuiness
Judge, Superior Court
Alameda County
1986–

1972
Hon. Gary M. Picetti
Judge, Municipal Court
Alameda County
1984–

1973
Hon. Jeffrey S. Allen
Judge, Municipal Court
Alameda County
1985–

1974
Hon. Larry J. Goodman
Judge, Superior Court
Alameda County
1984–

1974
Hon. Fernando Guzman
Judge, Juvenile Court
Clark County, Nevada
1980–

1974
Hon. Joanne C. Parrilli
Judge, Municipal Court
Alameda County
1985–

1974
Hon. Mary J. Theis
Associate Judge, Circuit Court
Cook County, Illinois
1983–

1975
Hon. Vincent T. Lechowick
Judge, Justice Court
Mendocino County
1979–

1975
Hon. Luis M. Villareal
Judge, Municipal Court
Solano County
1982–

1976
Hon. Martha Beckwith
Judge, District Court
Anchorage, Alaska
1984–

1978
Hon. Peggy F. Hora
Judge, Municipal Court
Alameda Court
1985–

USF SCHOOL OF LAW BAR PASS RATE CALIFORNIA STATE BAR EXAM FIRST-TIME TAKERS

(Based on available statistics)

The measure of a law school is not always its pass rate on the bar examination, but very few students enroll in law school expecting to fail the test after three years of study. The exam itself goes to the heart of a deep and abiding ambivalence that characterizes legal education in America: whether to teach the law as a practical vocation or as a field of intellectual concern. At times, the bar examiners have been accused of using the test simply to exclude large numbers of would-be lawyers and therefore maintain the exclusivity of the profession. At other times, the exam has been seen as a critical tool for protecting the public from less than qualified practitioners. At all times, the test has reflected not only the quality of education at a particular institution, but also the changing pool of law students and the varying particular concerns of the bar examiners. The record of USF graduates on the bar has influenced the history of the law school considerably.

	SPRING		FALL	
YEAR	NUMBER TESTED	PERCENT PASSED	NUMBER TESTED	PERCENT PASSED
1928			35	62.8%
1929	2	50.0%	35	60.0%
1930			41	48.7%
1931			18	44.0%
1932	11	00.0%	29	51.7%
1933	1	00.0%	32	34.4%
1934			33	33.3%
1935	3	00.0%	15	53.3%
1936	7	85.7%	17	58.8%
1937	5	20.0%	21	61.9%
1938	3	100.0%	11	72.7%
1939	2	100.0%	11	54.5%
1940				
1941			14	57.1%
1942			3	33.3%
1943			3	33.3%
1944				
1945	6	100.0%	9	66.7%
1946	2	100.0%	13	30.8%
1947	6	83.3%	23	73.9%
1948	25	84.0%	28	82.1%
1949	43	81.0%	42	61.9%
1950	15	53.3%	68	58.8%
1951	46	41.3%	58	37.9%
1952	20	50.0%	40	55.0%
1953	15	75.7%	30	60.0%
1954	9	66.7%	24	58.3%
1955	6	83.3%	28	92.9%
1956	3	100.0%	19	73.6%
1957	4	100.0%	22	72.7%

	SPRING		FALL	
YEAR	NUMBER TESTED	PERCENT PASSED	NUMBER TESTED	PERCENT PASSED
1958	2	50.0%	42	54.8%
1959			47	55.3%
1960	7	71.4%	41	73.1%
1961	2	100.0%	39	79.4%
1962	1	100.0%	35	85.7%
1963	3	100.0%	39	82.0%
1964	5	60.0%	38	65.8%
1965			55	69.1%
1966	4	100.0%	60	70.0%
1967	4	75.0%	60	76.7%
1968	3	66.7%	79	88.6%
1969				
1970			57	80.7%
1971	3	100.0%	78	83.3%
1972	3	100.0%	88	84.1%
1973	14	64.3%	173	74.0%
1974	29	75.9%	153	81.0%
1975	34	73.5%	150	71.3%
1976	48	58.0%	123	65.0%
1977	29	76.0%	161	64.0%
1978*			223	62.3%
1979	14	57.0%	171	75.0%
1980	24	67.0%	154	73.0%
1981	27	59.0%	169	71.0%
1982	24	33.0%	168	60.7%
1983	18	17.0%	170	70.6%
1984	18	56.0%	195	55.0%
1985	25	40.0%	168	49.0%
1986	18	33.0%	175	53.7%

*Spring and Fall figures combined.

NOTES

CHAPTER 1

1. Much of the information on the daily routine of law school days in the Grant Building comes from a group oral history project organized by Thomas Jordan and Dean Paul McKaskle. A transcript is available in the USF Archives. Participants included Vincent Compagno, Preston Devine, and Ed Molkenbuhr.
2. Ignatian, 1911, vol. no. 1, 48.
3. Michael Accolti, S.J., "A Memorial of the Journey to California," quoted in John Bernard McGloin, S.J., *Jesuits by the Golden Gate* (San Francisco; University of San Francisco, 1972), 1.
4. Anthony Maraschi, S.J., "A Relation of Facts Connected with the Foundation of St. Ignatius College of the Society of Jesus in San Francisco, California," quoted in McGloin, *Jesuits by the Golden Gate*, 5.
5. Henry Woods, S.J., "The Necessity of Establishing Professional Schools in Connexion with Our Colleges in California," 4. California Collection, 1004–VI, Archivum Romanum Societatis Iesu.
6. McGloin, *Jesuits by the Golden Gate*, 100.
7. *San Francisco Chronicle*, July 1, 1937.
8. David Wooster Taylor, *The Life of James Rolph, Jr.* (San Francisco; Committee for Publication of the Life of James Rolph, Jr., 1934).
9. Ibid., 53.

CHAPTER 2

1. Robert Burchell, *The San Francisco Irish: 1848–1880* (Berkeley; University of California Press, 1980), 3.
2. J.C. Bates, ed., *History of the Bench and Bar of California* (San Francisco; Bench and Bar Publishing Company, 1912), 748.
3. Robert Stevens, *Law School: Legal Education in America from the 1850s to the 1980s* (Chapel Hill; University of North Carolina Press, 1983), 75.
4. Ibid., 73.
5. Kenneth M. Johnson, *The Bar Association of San Francisco: The First Hundred Years* (San Francisco; The Bar Association of San Francisco, 1972), 72.
6. James P. Walsh, *San Francisco's Hallinan: Toughest Lawyer in Town* (Novato; Presidio Press, 1982), 29.
7. California Survey Committee, State Bar of California, *Report of the California Survey Committee* (San Francisco; The State Bar of California, 1933), 3.
8. McGloin, *Jesuits by the Golden Gate*, 152.

CHAPTER 3

1. McGloin, *Jesuits by the Golden Gate*, 101.
2. *State Bar Journal*, see relevant years.
3. *American Bar Association Journal*, vol. 9, no. 11, 728.
4. *State Bar Journal*, November 1935, 28.
5. State Bar of California, *Report of the California Survey Committee*, 2.
6. Ibid., 35
7. Ibid., 32–36.
8. Charles F. Carroll, S.J., "Some Observations on the Law School for 1934–35," March 8, 1934, University of San Francisco Archives (USFA).
9. Lewis Cassidy, letter to the Members of the Committee of Legal Education and Admissions to the Bar of the American Bar Association, June 19, 1936, 2, USFA.
10. Raymond T. Feely, letter to Rev. Harold E. Ring, January 17, 1935, 3, USFA.
11. Lewis Cassidy, letter to Raymond Feely, April 3, 1935, USFA.
12. Raymond Feely, letter to Rev. Harold E. Ring, April 11, 1935, USFA.
13. Lewis Cassidy, letter to the Members of the Committee of Legal Education and Admissions to the Bar of the American Bar Association, June 19, 1936, 7–8, USFA.

CHAPTER 4

1. Henry Woods, S.J., "The Necessity of Establishing Professional Schools in Connexion with Our Colleges in California," 15.
2. Ibid., 5–6.
3. Ibid., 17.
4. St. Ignatius University, *Bulletin*, 1912–1913 (San Francisco, 1912), 8.
5. Henry Woods, S.J., "The Necessity of Establishing Professional Schools in Connexion with Our Colleges in California," 11.
6. Lewis Cassidy, letter to the Members of the Committee of Legal Education and Admissions to the Bar of the American Bar Association, June 19, 1936, 4, USFA.
7. John G. Hervey, speech given before the Association of Jesuit Law Schools, December 29, 1954, USFA.
8. Raymond Feely, letter to Lewis Cassidy, April 11, 1935, 2, USFA.
9. Harold Ring, memorandum to John O'Reilly, May 25, 1936, USFA.
10. School of Law, University of San Francisco, *Announcement of the School of Law* (San Francisco, 1936), 19, USFA.
11. Charles H. Kinnane, *A First Book on Anglo-American Law* (Indianapolis; The Bobbs-Merrill Company, Inc., 1932), p. viii.
12. Ibid., p. x.
13. Charles H. Kinnane, "Report of the Dean of the School of Law," 1938, USFA.
14. Charles H. Kinnane, memorandum to William J. Dunne, October 12, 1938, 1, USFA.
15. Ibid., 2.
16. William J. Dunne, letter to Charles H. Kinnane, February 15, 1939, 1, USFA.

NOTES

CHAPTER 5

1. McGloin, *Jesuits by the Golden Gate*, 170.
2. Stevens, *Law School*, 161.
3. Edward A. Hogan, Jr. and Edward C. Menager, S.J., "Philosophy and Legal Thinking," *San Francisco Quarterly*, Spring–Summer 1940, 7.
4. Edward A. Hogan, Jr., "St. Thomas More in the World of Today," *San Francisco Quarterly*, Winter 1941, 12–13.
5. Hogan and Menager, "Philosophy and Legal Thinking," 6.
6. Edward A. Hogan, Jr., "The Fifth Decade of Federal Legislation in the Field of Labor Disputes," *Georgetown Law Journal*, December 1939, 362.
7. Thomas H. Watkins and Roger R. Olmsted, *Mirror of the Dream* (San Francisco; Scrimshaw Press, 1976), 248–249.
8. McGloin, *Jesuits by the Golden Gate*, 190.
9. Ibid., 174.
10. Henry Howard, unpublished memoirs.

CHAPTER 6

1. Joseph McClain, Jr., Thomas McDonald, and Sydney Post Simpson, *Legal Education and Admissions to the Bar in California* (San Francisco; The State Bar of California, 1949), 68.
2. William J. Dunne, letter to Edward A. Hogan, Jr., December 14, 1949, USFA.
3. Dunne and Miller correspondence, various pieces during the fall of 1949, USFA.
4. William J. Dunne, letter to Edward A. Hogan, Jr., December 14, 1949, USFA.
5. Edward A. Hogan, Jr., letter to William J. Dunne, December 20, 1949, USFA.
6. Vernon X. Miller, telegram and letter to William J. Dunne, February 8, 1950, USFA.
7. McClain, McDonald, and Simpson, *Legal Education and Admissions to the Bar in California*, 70.
8. Ibid., 72.
9. Ibid., 72.
10. McGloin, *Jesuits by the Golden Gate, 193.*
11. Thomas Garden Barnes, *Hastings College of the Law: The First Century* (San Francisco; Hastings College of the Law, 1978), 307–321.

CHAPTER 7

1. Ignatius M. Wilkinson, letter to William J. Dunne, July 14, 1949, USFA.
2. Vernon X. Miller, "Memorandum to All Faculty Members," January 7, 1952, USFA.
3. The Student Committee, letter to William J. Dunne, February 13, 1953, USFA.
4. Raymond T. Feely, letter to Vernon X. Miller, January 29, 1954, USFA.
5. Vernon X. Miller, letter to William J. Dunne, July 10, 1953, USFA.
6. Vernon X. Miller, letter to William J. Dunne, June 8, 1954, USFA.
7. McGloin, *Jesuits by the Golden Gate*, 232.

CHAPTER 8

1. Barnes, *Hastings College of the Law*, 388–389.
2. Interview with Frank Walsh, November 7, 1986.
3. Interview with Thomas Jordan, November 10, 1986.
4. John Connolly, S.J., *USF Alumnus*, October/November 1960, 3.
5. Interview with Thomas Jordan, November 10, 1986.
6. Stevens, *Law School*, 207.
7. Ibid.
8. John G. Hervey, speech given before the Association of Jesuit Law Schools, December 29, 1954, 3, USFA.
9. *San Francisco News-Call-Bulletin*, "Priest Criticizes 'Faceless' Firms," September 27, 1962.
10. Herman Phleger, "The Lawyer in a Challenging World," *Principal Addresses: The Dedication of Kendrick Hall, University of San Francisco, School of Law* (San Francisco; University of San Francisco, 1962), 5.
11. Robert F. Kennedy, speech given by telephone, September 29, 1962, *Principal Addresses: The Dedication of Kendrick Hall, University of San Francisco, School of Law* (San Francisco; University of San Francisco, 1962), 10.

CHAPTER 9

1. Lewis H. Butler, speech reprinted, *USF Alumnus*, April 1970, 2.
2. Quoted in William E. Leuchtenburg, ed., *The Unfinished Century: America Since 1900* (Boston; Little, Brown and Company, 1973), 919.
3. Interview with Albert Jonsen, December 9, 1986.
4. Thomas McCarthy, *Forum*, April 1970, 4.
5. Russell Berti, "B & B," *Forum*, October 29, 1970, 1.
6. *USF Alumnus*, "Around Campus," Autumn 1971, 12.
7. C. Delos Putz, "Letters to the Editor," *Forum*, December 1971, 3.
8. University of San Francisco, School of Law, *Response of the University of San Francisco School of Law to the ABA-AALS Accreditation Questionaire*, March 1973, 6, USFA.
9. Anne Kane, "Law School's Interests Guaranteed by University," *Forum*, November 19, 1973, 1, 3.
10. William McInnes, "USF Law School: 'Where We Are... Where We Are Going,'" *Forum*, March 4, 1974, 1.
11. Interview with C. Delos Putz, October 26, 1986.

CHAPTER 10

1. Stevens, *Law School*, 238–243.
2. *Forum*, "300 Demonstrate at USF," February 23, 1978, 1.
3. Lyn Powers, "We Finally Got One," *Forum*, February 4, 1981, 1.
4. *Report of the Dean to the University of San Francisco School of Law Assembly* (1984 and 1986), USFA.
5. Interview with David Ratner, October 31, 1986.
6. Ibid.

INDEX